Office
Warfare

Also by
Charles Peattie and Russell Taylor
and published by Headline

ALEX CALLS THE SHOTS

Office Warfare

Michael Becket

with
Alex cartoons
by
Charles Peattie
and Russell Taylor

HEADLINE

Text copyright © 1993 Michael Becket
Cartoons copyright © 1993 Charles Peattie and Russell Taylor

First published in 1993 by HEADLINE BOOK PUBLISHING

The right of Michael Becket, Charles Peattie and Russell Taylor to be
identified as the authors of the work has been asserted by them in
accordance with the Copyright, Designs and Patents Act 1988

10 9 8 7 6 5 4 3 2 1

British Library Cataloguing in Publication Data
Becket, Michael Ivan H.
Office Warfare: Executive Survival Guide
I. Title II. Peattie, Charles
III. Taylor. Russell
658.4

ISBN 0-7472-0946-4 (hardback)
ISBN 0 7472 7870 9 (softback)

Design and computer page make up by Tony and Penny Mills

Printed and bound in Great Britain by
BPCC Hazell Books Ltd
Member of BPCC Ltd

HEADLINE BOOK PUBLISHING
A division of Hodder Headline PLC
Headline House
79 Great Titchfield Street
London W1P 7FN

Contents

Introduction

Rambo had it easy – at least by comparison with those in the world of business. He knew who the enemies were and had only to kill them, and that was the end of it. In commerce you fight not only competing companies but also thrusting colleagues in the battle for supremacy and survival, and struggle to keep your staff marshalled continuously for best performance. There is psychological warfare, duplicity and treachery. And none of the combatants is beaten for good: the struggle continues.

What is it all for? Money and power. Only losers tell you money can't buy happiness. At the very least it makes misery more comfortable. In fact it buys most things that can make you happy, from extra health care to the company of entertaining people. And the gaps left by money are filled by power. Little wonder then that executives struggle daily for a greater share of the cash going. The weapons in this are a firm grip on reality, alertness, and knowledge of how the system really works.

To make the organisation work for you requires an understanding of the strategies and aims of the people in it and how to manoeuvre them into helping you.

This book lays out the tactics on each of the main campaigns, from recruitment to retirement; from pay rises to motivating your staff. By showing how the system works this guide will help managers not only to survive corporate wars but to channel ambition into tactics that produce results.

The use of `he' is merely to avoid long and clumsy wording – the advice is directed at least as much towards women.

1

Recruitment

The longer the title, the less important the job

Nobody is ever going to recruit the right people – if the candidates were that wonderful why on earth would they be prepared to take on routine jobs working for someone else? Ideal candidates have talents that mean they would not be submitting themselves to the indignities of job applications. They would be away collecting their Nobel prizes or nipping off to the Caribbean to buy their own islands for the holidays. So reconcile yourself to making the best of who there is.

On top of that there is a similar set of contradictions in what abilities almost any job requires. It is as well to realise from the start that what you are asking for is a mass of paradoxes: the people need initiatives but must comply with the organisation's methods and rules; they must be intelligent yet do routine work for low pay; they must be capable but available; they must be young but experienced. It sounds like a nasty case of schizophrenia.

Recessions make recruiters think they are so brilliant they can defy gravity. When there is high unemployment they can offer low wages and still manage to find bright and energetic people to do the work and eventually they come to think it is their own recruiting skill that has worked the trick. Lulled by bouts of high jobless levels they think it will always be a breeze. In fact, in only a few years it could start turning quite nasty.

With the recent fall in the birth rate there will be a shortage of young people in a few years' time so finding the right people is going to become much more competitive.[1]

I Finding someone

So stop. Wait. Think. Before dashing off frantically to hire someone, pause a moment. There may be other ways round the problem and they could produce some useful survival strategies. The first question to ask is: why hire someone at all. It is just as possible the job could be done by existing staff or scrapped altogether. If the answer is that somebody really does have to be taken on the second question·is: what precisely do we want the new recruit to do, and of course why. A careful description will in turn produce the third question: what sort of person could do that job. This in turn will suggest the fourth question: what is the best way of finding that person.

Why are you recruiting?
Much of the recruitment in anything but the tiniest organisation comes from empire building. From the company's view and, if you happen to be a senior executive, from your view, this is not only unjustifiable but must be stopped to keep the finances in line. Some of it comes from genuine expansion of work, but then only the profits will provide a validation for that.

Even if that sort of hiring is stopped you cannot afford to relax. Replacing existing people may not really be necessary either.

The justification for getting extra people is that there is too much work for those already there. If people worked as hard as they pretend to, few would survive to see forty. Even if they really are putting in a lot of effort it is seldom to much effect. Making the work simpler and the department more efficient might be more constructive.

Many jobs are done only because they have always been done. One

3

useful wheeze is to get bright young executives within their first three months at the company to provide a confidential analysis to the top people of how procedures can be simplified, routines rationalised and work eliminated. After that time new people are assimilated, they form friendships which they do not want to betray, and they lose the shock of novelty.

Tactics for executives Recruiting is power. There are two main reasons for hiring staff – replacement and addition – and both have enormous potential for creating a power base. Of course in your department or section every person leaving must be immediately replaced, at least by somebody better but preferably by two people. The same does not apply throughout a company; at least not from where you are sniping.

One devious ploy is to suggest to someone senior that the other section does not really need the replacement (much less extra) staff and if it is having such difficulty coping with the work, your section will take it on instead. You will get a reputation for keen enterprise that will not be dented when eight months later you demand more staff to cope with the heavy extra workload.

To be fair not all increases in staffing are symptoms of empire building, but most are. Most managers reckon to be overworked, and it takes a conscientious man to tell whether he is tired or just plain lazy.

Parkinson's Law said `work expands so as to fill the time available for its completion'.[2] In fact good tactics demonstrate time is never quite sufficient for the work to be done and any ambitious manager must allow for the future when more and better work will be expected, by building up staff.

Tactics for senior managers   It is safe to assume most executives are working on that principle. It might be useful at this stage therefore to propose some Becket Laws of Staffing:

- all organisations are overstaffed
- staff grows faster than the work
- the largest growth is in the least productive sections
- new functions are always being created
- everybody is overworked

It follows that a well-managed organisation will insist that every three years it cuts the numbers on the payroll by ten per cent. That includes the personnel department, which is probably superfluous in any case.

Incidentally, even if a personnel department is retained, it should certainly not be trusted with the Milk Round. The people best suited for finding able young enthusiasts are the ones actually doing the work, since they do not deal in questionnaires and corporate images but can explain at first hand precisely what the job entails and can fire prospective recruits with the fun of the work.

The departments which have been growing fastest need to be cut the most, no matter how cleverly they have put up a case against it, because they have almost certainly built extra fat into the structure in anticipation of the regular and predictable restrictions instituted by the board at moments of panic.

Cuts will be met with squeals of anguish and howls of protest. The better in-fighters will also put up elaborate cases showing work is being skimped or being left undone. The volume of noise is an indication of the time and ability to fight rather than of genuine need. There could be eight reasons for claims of being overworked:

- as justification for not doing the job properly
- a puritan work ethic which jabs some executives with constant guilt
- gross inefficiency in the way the work is being done
- insufficient concentration or insecurity to ask for assistance to share the load
- inability to delegate
- incompetent subordinates
- the executive is just not up to the job
- the company itself is blatantly exploitative in a restricted labour market

It is clear that only the last of these has any basis in real effort. To judge therefore whether someone really does need to be hired see first if:[3]

- the job being done is really necessary
- the work justifies a full-time person, or could be done part time
- a temp could manage on a casual basis
- it is possible to reorganise to spread the work among existing staff or to shift an under-utilised worker from another section
- existing people can work a little longer – more overtime
- the task can be mechanised, automated or simplified
- the work can be subcontracted at a true cost lower than in-house staff

What is the job to be done?
Do not take the job specification merely as a description of the present or previous incumbent. Such shackles not only stifle initiative but prevent the organisation adapting. If the recruit is any good, the job will be altered by his capabilities and inclination, so it is sensible to allow for that from the start.

6

Guess I was wrong about you – you're not such an asshole after all – No, you were right – I'm just your kinda asshole

What sort of person is needed?
You can tell a lot about a manager from the quality of his subordinates.

Tactics for executives   Recruiting second-raters may ensure they do not fight to displace their boss and that they do not provide distraction from one's own brilliance. On the other hand duffers will be little help in producing the sort of outstanding results that could help that manager get promoted.

It makes sense, therefore, to get the best possible people even if at first they look like competitors for the top job. A bit of crafty manipulation, some clever politicking, and taking credit for the department's performance will ensure the ones on top stay there. As Leo Rosten said 'First-rate people hire first-rate people; second-rate people hire third-rate people'.

The job specifications will themselves suggest the type of person needed, but unless the recruiters write down something at the beginning of the interview they will be swept along by the charm of the interviewee. Just as before going to an auction you should write the maximum price in the catalogue margin to prevent being carried away by the lights and the music, so a list of required characteristics will focus the interviewer's minds. In both cases exceptional circumstances may bend the rules but this will usually be regretted later.

How to find the right person
Where you find ideal people is the real problem. Advertising is all very well for salesmen, machine operators, and clerks, but decent secretaries come from agencies and middle to top managers have to be hunted down individually (assuming there is no one suitable for promotion – see **Promotion**).

Getting a headhunter to do the job is subcontracting out a task most people could do at least as well in-house. What does a headhunter do when given the objective of finding a production director for a toothbrush maker? Exactly what any logical person would do: contact someone knowledgeable about the industry and ask who is good on the production side.

But presumably the recruiting company is already in toothbrush making and so knows more about the industry and more people in it (including trade press and stockbrokers' analysts) than any London smoothie. The company can also sift applicants more efficiently and knows the going rate for the job.

The main advantage of using headhunters is to maintain anonymity. You do not want the present finance director nervously padding himself with an overstuffed pension because he has glimpsed a dagger being sharpened for his back, and you do not want the sales manager offering to take the star performers to a competitor when he discovers candidates being interviewed for his job. It is tactless to allow a senior executive to discover that all is not well by finding his job advertised in the national press.

It used to be said the ideal job advertisement draws a single applicant: the perfect one. If there were more, either the salary offered was too high or too much was being spent on publicising the vacancy, or both. But that adage dates from the days of lower unemployment. When the labour market tightens again it may recur but for the time being even lavatory cleaning jobs draw hundreds of PhD applicants, so selection is a painful process.

II Selection methods

Selection techniques are delightfully unreliable. There is only a limited range

of techniques for screening and any intelligent and determined goat can fool a personnel manager into thinking him a sheep. But that is all right – after all, any organisation can do with a few mavericks bright enough to elude detection when it suits them. The trouble is the system lets in not only the occasional goat but wolves as well.

You don't get a second chance to make a first impression

For the sake of convenience selection techniques can probably be grouped under five main headings:

- interviews
- personality tests
- intelligence and aptitude tests
- other, 'fringe' methods
- previous performance

Interviews

Interviewing depends almost wholly on the interviewer being better at judging character than the candidate is at acting, yet the evidence is that most employers would not be able to pick out a homicidal werewolf from a parade of Ursuline nuns.

Unhappily it is an all too human weakness to imagine one is a good judge of character though all the available evidence shows most managers range from the inept to the useless.[4] Interviewers make up their minds about the candidate from the application form or at best in the first five minutes of the interview, and the rest of the time is spent looking for evidence to justify that conclusion.

Being subjective, the system leads to predictably varied reactions to the same person. It has also proved to be a rotten predictor of performance. Still, presumably one has to have it all the same, if only to exchange factual information.

What sets off the metal detector first? The lead in your ass or the shit in your brains?

Personality tests

There are 'objective' tests such as personality profiles. A large number of questionnaires is available but the main thrust of them all is much the same. Personality tests can be revealing but only if the subject has not taken one before, knows nothing of psychology or sociology, and is not very bright.

Each test asks hundreds of questions on the fatuous principle respondents will not spot the same question from a different angle and so liars will be tripped up. In fact not only is it easy to remember but an intelligent applicant merely takes on the personality the organisation presumably wants for the job and answers the questions appropriately.

The questions themselves probe deep into the guilty psyche with such subtle interrogations as 'Would you rather be a lumberjack or a ballet dancer?'. The answer 'No' is not acceptable. The shortcomings of such systems are all too obvious:

- nobody is sure what balance of characteristics is best for any job
- any halfwit can manipulate even the most elaborate tests
- most of the tested traits are wholly irrelevant
- the various tests disagree about what they find

Intelligence tests

Intelligence tests on the other hand test the ability to take intelligence tests.[5] For top jobs it is not just that intelligence may be beside the point,[6] but that people applying may get just a mite stroppy if their PhD and long career were not considered evidence of being able to tie their own shoelaces.[7]

There are several different types of intelligence. For instance:

Actions speak louder than words

- verbal
- numerical
- problem–solving
- ability to abstract
- ability to profit from experience
- absorption of data
- adaptability

Considering there is no generally agreed definition of intelligence it is wonderful the experts managed to devise tests for it some ninety years ago.[8]

Instead of intelligence, one could test for various aptitudes – fine for production workers, but finding an appropriate one for managers would be tricky.

Other tests
Graphology is one of the more fringe or indirect methods for screening applicants. It differs from astrology, palmistry and tea-leaf reading in having some intellectually plausible basis. But being non-quantified there are few good practitioners about and some produce descriptions with all the penetrating insight and erudition of a newspaper horoscope.

Prediction
The best predictor of performance according to all the attempts at systematic research is an established record of success. The only problem is that it is surprisingly difficult to establish. For instance, was a sales director apparently wonderful only because he happened to have an outstanding salesman at the time, and did a company prosper under a managing director only because his predecessor had instituted policies which had flowered?

Tactics for executives If personality tests are obligatory you need to work

out what sort of person the company is likely to want for the job – aggressive, cooperative, self-reliant, sympathetic or whatever – and answer the questions in that persona. But it is probably wisest to avoid organisations with such superstitious beliefs.

At interviews never just answer a question. There are more important considerations than the apparent reply: why are they asking a particular question? What is the relationship between the people on the panel and hence what sort of response do different ones require? What assumptions lie behind the question? Is this really the right question in the circumstances?

Such an approach not only commits you to nothing, it makes you sound penetrating and perceptive, and makes it impossible to compare you with the other applicants.

III Procedure

Given so many hurdles to jump how is the poor bewildered recruiter to find the right person? He cannot, but by God he had better go through some pretty careful motions so if the one who gets the job turns out to be a homicidal maniac, professional spy, or elaborate embezzler, he can prove the procedures were right.

The selection procedure has gone way beyond such humble ambitions as finding the appropriate person for the job. There are so many laws, rules, regulations and constraints that finding someone competent is the least of the problems. At one time it was relatively simple: one had merely to justify to one's boss that the person chosen could perform the job. Now the lawyers and the state are watching as well.

Tactics for executives   Any manager who is actually going to take on the responsibility for hiring someone (assuming the personnel department cannot be given any blame) had better start early on by building up a defensive armour for later attacks. There is a safety procedure to reduce the risk of choosing someone entirely unsuitable and at the very simplest this means going through a series of checks:

- application forms
- interview
- tests
- references

Selectors must not discriminate from or to anything or anybody. Even nepotism is being criticised. Like all negatives, absence of prejudice is impossible to prove. Picking a young, white, middle-class man can provoke a torrent of abuse and interrogation about bias against women, the old, the crippled, blacks and Asians, plus queries about views on homosexuality, dress preferences, and class. Prepare the case against campaigners well in advance.

On the other hand to hell with the law – what is a company doing settling for anything but the best? If the best applicant is female it takes a peculiar form of financial suicide to pick a male.

Somehow even prolonged public vilification seems not to have stopped men at the top getting the prettiest or the most efficient secretary (depending on preference and their wives' intervention).

But bear in mind the problem has not gone away just by sensibly impartial recruiting. When the going gets rough and the strains begin to show, vicious deep prejudices begin to surface. Bias remains, but as was recently pointed out, if it is so easy for women to sleep their way to the top, how come so few get there?

Gizza job!   *References*

Only an idiot would give as a referee somebody who would let on about the sentences for GBH and embezzlement, or about being variously sacked for indecent exposure, drunkenness, and gross dereliction of duty. All the same, it is worth taking them up, for two reasons. Firstly, the applicant may just be bluffing. Perhaps the Archbishop of York, the Duke of Buccleuch and David Sainsbury are not lifelong chums.

It is astonishing, but complete ignoramuses have talked their way into consultancies at major teaching hospitals because nobody bothered to check their impressive references. Is it really likely no such cons have succeeded in the private sector without the hoo-ha?

Secondly, people prefer being honest. So do not write to referees but ring them up, or better still meet. Instead of the anodyne formula everybody puts into a letter of reference, odd little hints, suggestions and truths emerge when people are on no permanent record.

IV How to land a job

Companies are stuck with what we might well call the Columbus conundrum: he didn't know where he was going, didn't know where he was when he got there, and didn't know where he had been when he got back. In the same way, recruiters have little idea of what they are looking for, do not know how to discriminate between applicants, have not the faintest notion of what they have found, and have scant appreciation of how to judge if the person picked performs as required.

Tactics for executives All this provides candidates with a puzzle and an opportunity. A puzzle because they have to fit a picture which is at best hazy, and an opportunity because an uncertain recruiter can be persuaded that across the desk is the executive of the company's dreams.

One approach is classical games theory. This was first set out methodically some fifty years ago by mathematician John von Neumann and Oskar Morgenstern, and everything since then has merely elaborated or refined the original clean vision.[9]

It depends on an unemotional evaluation of alternative strategies open to a competitor or opponent, working out one's responses to each, and mathematically weighing the results. The main weakness of games theory is that it assumes the opponent is a rational person maximising advantages to produce the best outcome. Any sensible player will allow for the emotional bias that often prevents people from taking the best option.

The main point is that from your very first move you are working from a set of assumptions about what the other side wants or expects.[10] Put yourself in the opponent's shoes and devise the optimum reaction to each potential move. The theory forms the basis for most battles and operates throughout corporate life.

One commonly used example shows how it can be applied.[11] Two men in jail are each offered the same deal: if you confess to robbery and your associate does not, you will be released and he will get a long sentence, and vice versa if he confesses and you do not. If both confess to robbery the sentence will be only moderately long. If neither confesses both will get only a light sentence for vagrancy. Clearly both would be better off if neither confessed, but each would be sensible if he assumed the other would be

15

Wait till they get a load of me

pursuing not what is collectively better, or better for society, or any of that hogwash, but would be trying to get himself the best available deal. In other words, he will do a similar calculation and confess.

Much of corporate tactics for executives derives from this.

Curriculum vitae

There is little point in providing a CV that lists achievements from a Nobel prize upwards, that demonstrates the compassion of a saint, the learning of a collegefull of dons, and with a versatility encompassing concert-standard violin playing through research papers in quantum physics to amateur brain surgery. This would just scare any prospective boss silly.

The obvious aim for a candidate is to accord with the recruiting manager's predispositions. CVs, like all history, are flexible interpretations.

As in relations with the Inland Revenue however it is unwise to tell an outright lie – at least not one that can be shown to be an intentional falsehood. Claiming to have been a cardiovascular consultant at St Georges when your medical knowledge derives solely from the advice pages of Woman's Own, is probably unwise. Similarly, although most companies will not bother to check whether you really did get a starred first from Balliol and a PhD from MIT, they just might.

A certain latitude for hyperbole is permissible. A holiday job as a filing clerk at an advertising agency may be distorted slightly to demonstrate experience in interpreting market research data; the briefest transit through the sales department during a management trainee course can be interpreted as expertise.

Performance

When the going gets tough, the tough get going

Survival depends on performance. So to be a survivor either you hit the targets that have been set or move the target to where you have actually hit. The obvious moral of that is to make sure people in competition with you in the organisation are set viciously precise goals (mainly by suggestions to the bosses), tough but precisely definable targets are given to the people below you, while your own work is left creatively fluid.

The people working to you will provide elaborate and eloquent conviction that their work cannot possibly be measured; that although it is invaluable it certainly cannot be quantified. To which the correct answer is: anything that cannot be counted and calculated is almost certainly not invaluable but valueless. Whatever exists exists in some quantity and can therefore be measured. This applies especially to people's performance.

It may not be easy, it is often inconvenient or even embarrassing, but some criterion can be set for every job from lathe operator to archbishop, from foreign exchange dealer to export manager, from barrister to purchasing clerk, and from neurosurgeon to whore. With no specific way of measuring you cannot set targets, which means you cannot tell if someone is doing well. And without that you have little idea of whether the company is running effectively, and appropriate rewards and punishments are impossible.

Business depends on people; good organisations depend on good people. Bonuses, promotions, and firings stem from finding and rewarding those good ones and getting shot of the useless ones.

I Setting targets

There is little problem with defining or assessing the performance of a company. Pre-tax profits (or whatever it is the new accounting regulations are supposed to show), and dividends are effective indicators. There are of course many other esoteric figures and ratios from return on investment and shareholders' funds, to profit as ratio of capital or sales, gearing, stock-turnover rate, and so on, but these are for specialists.

If profits fall and dividends are cut stand by for trouble. This is especially true if they fall 'unexpectedly' – City jargon for not having warned the analysts of the results being published. If you do drop the hint (being careful not to be found out by the stock exchange authorities) analysts can put out reports predicting trouble, and so seem clever. Without such face-savers analysts are shown up for the useless readers of company reports most of them are and their consequent rage is terrifying to behold.

The same applies to the press. Both analysts and journalists will throw elaborate tantrums and hurl at the company the bitter recriminations and malice of rejected lovers if they are seen to be ignorant.

All this hammering from stockbrokers' circulars and the press knocks the share price and the company is vulnerable to insolvency or takeover; they are equally bad since executives are liable to lose their jobs.

Tactics for senior managers　Two morals emerge from this. Firstly, you should know when the results for the current year are going to be dire and that means good management accounts. Secondly, leak the bad news gently to the main stockbrokers and the largest shareholders to prepare them for the worst. But do it carefully because this is against the stock exchange rules.

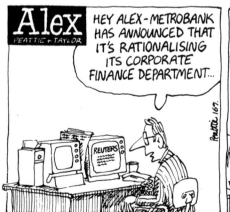

If you don't drive your business you will be driven out of business

In addition, some companies may want to grow, some to diversify, some want an international base, some want to go public, some want to go back to being private again, some want to shift the structure sideways into a slightly different sort of business, and so on.

First have a clear, identifiable goal, said Aristotle, then have the means to achieve it – knowledge, money, material and methods – and third, adjust your means to your goal.

It sounds all right when you say it quickly, but in practice it is a bit tougher than that makes it sound. Setting even what seems like straightforward physical targets is not easy. There is the classic example of the Russian nail factory which had been set a production target by its Soviet commissars of so many hundredweight of nails a month. So it produced only nails weighing a pound and a half each. Having got wise, the commissars revised the measure of success to numbers of output, only to receive millions of nails, each an eighth of an inch long.

When there is no physical output to count the task is even harder. Measuring the effort of solicitors or sewermen, architects or archbishops is not easy. But it can be done. And it should be done. This is not to say that everybody is expected to be on piece-work, but some assessment is vital.

Evaluation should start on the day an employee joins to see if juniors, articled clerks, trainees, graduate intake, and so on are up to the mark, are fitting in, learning adequately, and worth keeping on. It makes sense to discover this in under two years as sacking employees becomes expensive after that (see **Discipline**).

If you are a shrewd manager you will build in as one of the targets the need to get better. Whatever the criterion – or even without any specific

criterion – if your staff realise they are expected to improve both their own performance and the work of their sections you are likely to start looking pretty good.

This is especially important in bureaucracies, which are amazingly resistant to pressure. Any major organisation with more than fifty office staff faces an entrenched bureaucracy intent on growth at best but at the very least a vigorous survival. To fight this demands a circuitous approach. Bureaucrats are intransigent in the face of efforts to prune their private baronies, as you would expect.

One man's red tape is another man's system

There is no kudos for a brave decision but every excuse for a safe one, so it is hardly surprising most managers opt for the defensible rather than the best policy. Annual assessments do not gauge the degree by which efficiency has been increased, but do check for soundness and reliability, so it makes eminent sense to avoid rocking the boat.

Describing the problem suggests the solutions. If you want to encourage a characteristic, you reward it. It is no good saying you want daring, ideas and energy if what you reward and promote is conservative time-serving. Employees are pretty quick to spot the difference between word and action. And they will always react to the action.

Tactics for executives   If you want the people working to you to produce improvements then tell them that is what is needed. If there are specific areas where things could be done better, say so; if the whole level of performance needs to be improved, explain that; and if what you really want are suggestions for ways to make the outfit more efficient or faster or whatever, tell them that too.

Secondly do not slap them down if some suggestions are less than brilliant or original, and don't be too hard if after a trial they don't work. As Fabius Maximus spotted some seventeen hundred years ago, `Avoiding mistakes in great enterprises is beyond men's abilities.'[1] People are very easily discouraged, and if you start pouring scorn on a second-rate notion you will probably never hear about it when that person has a brilliant idea. It is also likely to deter the others from stepping out of line if all they get in return is a spit in the eye.

Thirdly, reward the ones who provide what you want with praise, money and promotion.

The way to promotion and visible success is to have a steadily growing empire, if your boss has not been shrewd enough to set targets to prevent that. One way is to ensure the targets being set for your section seem to add functions and enormous volumes of work which in turn require you to recruit extra staff.

Despite that it is wise to demonstrate to the boss at times throughout the year that everybody – including of course yourself – is working flat out. It might be wise to hint in private that you are worried that some of the staff may have to skimp on some of the work (pick the ones dearest to his heart) unless they get some help. You of course are fine, despite working those hours.

To demonstrate those hours a variety of ploys are useful. The phone off the hook, an open pen on a notepad with some scribbles on and the jacket over the back of the chair show that you have just popped out for some information. Another useful tip is to take off your jacket with the coat as you come in at some far corner of the office by the entrance, so that by the time you are walking in to your desk in the morning you are already in shirt-

sleeves as if you had been working for hours.

It is also a useful ploy somehow to have your section included in the targets set for larger groupings or the company as a whole. That means the future of your section is seen as vital for the health of the rest of the organisation. That ensures you are listened to, quite apart from attracting the resources you need – not for the work but for your prestige.

The trouble with the rat race is that even if you win, you're still a rat

II Appraisal

Nobody said managing would be easy. Easy jobs are for underpaid wimps. Appraising in the sense of judging and hence forecasting performance is one of the harder aspects of the job and it would seem even the experts fall down at it. Not just the obvious people you would expect to fail like stockbrokers, not just amateurs and untutored managers, not just hapless investors, but the ones who have been acknowledged as world masters.

For instance, *In Search of Excellence* by Tom Peters and Robert Waterman [2] has been one of the most successful management books ever published and it provoked a noisome fleet of other titles slipstreaming it by putting 'excellent' in the title. Yet two-thirds of the forty-three companies which received the accolade in the original volume turned out to be rather less than wonderful as they floundered in the changes of the subsequent ten years, unable to cope with shifting economic circumstances. Probably there is only one company left from the original list which still lives up to the full billing.

They got it wrong. Perhaps it was disillusion with his prophetic powers that persuaded Tom Peters to start his next book with the words 'There are no excellent companies'.

Certainly in any assessment you should leave some element to chance

and serendipity. It is a well-established maxim that in business as 'in war you must always leave room for strokes of fortune and accidents'.[3] Executives still need to devise tests that tell them whether their own sections and the sub-groups below them are doing well.

Peters did however give some sound, if hardly revolutionary, advice:

- cut back on headquarters' staff
- concentrate on the customers' wants
- stick to the trade you know
- foster innovation
- encourage management that is up and doing

Most of us could add to the list without much difficulty[4] if we stopped to think. Like those purveyors of dreams – the writers who put together books with lists of successful people with sets of hints on how to emulate them – we can all sit down with a share price page and see which companies are highly rated and then try to work out what they have in common.

One obvious characteristic is flexibility, as every recent management book points out. These things move in fashions. Twenty years ago the rage was all for management-by-objectives and open and sensitive bosses; now the slogans proclaim creativity, encouragement of change, adaptable organisations, and concentration on innovation.

In sum the lessons of the latest batch of gurus can be summed up as: there is no such thing as a right organisation or approach since we live in chaotic times, so the survivor is the one that spots the opportunities and is alert enough to change in time.[5]

Although most companies have remained as stubbornly inflexible as

they always were their brighter executives at least now make token obeisance to the new orthodoxy.

It comes as no surprise that companies which fail to set targets and cannot decide on the criteria for individual success are pretty sloppy about the way they assess performance.

Tactics for executives For managers there is in fact a sense in keeping an eye on how people are doing even without such goals, if only from vulgar curiosity and as ammunition for later strategic moves. For instance, appraisal can be to:

- improve performance
- tell people how their bosses see them and what they expect of them
- provide encouragement
- identify training needs
- spot rising stars
- give pay rises

Even that briefest of lists shows all too painfully that the process splits the manager doing the job down the middle – having to be simultaneously helper and judge. It cannot be done properly as clearly the two roles conflict.[6] No sane employee is going to open his heart and ask for assistance and advice for problems if that could jeopardise the chances of getting a pay rise. The fail-safe course is obviously to induce approval.

It is certainly true most people are flattered to be asked for advice, and one's boss is not immune to such manipulation, but the moment and the subject have to be carefully chosen. A highly specialist problem in which

the boss is an acknowledged expert can well be discussed briefly even if you know the answer perfectly well, to allow an elaborate display of erudition and expertise. A suitably open-mouthed admiration signifies veneration and the brief process is concluded with profuse thanks.

That is very different from confessing to serious difficulties in one's work, and would certainly not be aired at a time of a formal interview about one's career. Unless, that is, you were angling to get on the short-list for redundancy. It is certainly not the recommended way to impress one's boss.

People who have been watching the process reckon the safest course for both sides is to leave personal advice to social workers and stick to a chat about performance, however defined.[7] Just because the boss has an annual chat with each subordinate – perhaps to discuss why his superiors are keeping too tight a control on the purse-strings to allow a decent rise this time – it does not mean the boss is also the one who carried out the appraisal that provided the background for this uncomfortable debate.

The appraisers

Bite the dust, sucker

The choice of who can do an annual summary of each person's work lies between:

- the immediate superior
- the superior's boss
- somebody from personnel department
- oneself for a sort of self-assessment
- colleagues

The first has the advantage of knowing the person and work so the process

becomes merely a formal extension of what should be continuous feedback, but on a more rigorous basis.[8] It allows a shrewd manager to nudge the competing subordinates into the directions needed. The pushy young executive who has been slagging you off to the rest of the management in a clear attempt to replace you in the job can be slapped down with all the force of indirection: merely a hint that he has obviously not settled happily into his work in the department, or that he is clearly having difficulty adjusting to the structure, should work wonders. The warning is given even greater force by the size of a pay increment.

Some managers use appraisals as a way of setting the various young Turks against each other in the hope they will spend so much time warring with each other they will not have time left to plot their boss's downfall. If caught at it such managers call it fomenting creative tension.

The sweetest word in the English language is revenge

If you are one of the executives on the receiving end of this tactic, you can use a very easy counter. Have a quiet private chat with each of the others who will have been set to war with you, and explain what the boss has said. It is permissible to exaggerate mildly and to make explicit what were veiled hints at the original interview, but do not overplay your hand – all you are trying to do is to show the boss to be a devious bastard who is trying to do down the executive you are warning.

With each one of your competitors apprised of the dirty ruse being used against them (each will take it as a personal affront) they will cooperate in hating the boss and working towards demise. With careful guidance and the occasional well-placed suggestion this can eliminate the competition and allow you to slip past on the outside.

Appraisal by the next grade up, the so-called grandfather assessment,

provides greater detachment and removes precisely this sort of self-interested back-biting. In picking people for promotion the wider view also allows a useful comparison across several groups or departments.

Appraisal by the personnel department is far too impersonal and is seldom used. Self-assessment depends on how it is used.[9] Francis Bacon said 'Praise yourself daringly, something always sticks' which is one of the handicaps of this method.[10] On the other hand when employees realise the self-description notes will be used at subsequent discussions, they become amazingly more modest and a touch more realistic.

Colleagues know best of all how well an individual performs, so their ratings could be both knowledgeable and reliable.[11] They know precisely who masks spectacular indolence with artistic simulations of fervent activity; they know who is trying to seduce whom and when it succeeds; they know who is good at the work but so busy getting on with it that nobody notices; and they know who is politicking and at what level.

Live fast, die young, and leave a good-looking corpse

Such reports would be wonderful but are seldom used. The two main reasons are that even if several overlapping assessments are taken into account it is hard to filter out the self-serving bias in what is said, and there is quite often a reluctance to sneak to management on even an unpopular worker. If the employee has charm then probably no amount of stupidity or intemperate sloth would be revealed except by the one jealous colleague who would then stand out and be called unreliable.

The further up the ladder one gets, the harder it is to judge how well somebody is doing. Yet it is at this elevated level that performance is notoriously variable, with the top people most wayward of all, and it is precisely here than an ability to spot the duds is most important.

One problem with appraisals is their acknowledged inability to show the

different patterns of achievement: we have all seen prodigies who rose like a rocket and fell like the stick. Hardly surprising, then, that the phrase 'burnt-out' is used.

Quite often the public doom of these people is sealed when performance fails precisely in those areas where the earlier work had been brilliant. Smugness and arrogance set in all too easily. The Greeks called it hubris which is the pride born of disregarding the limits of human ability and hence defiance of the gods. Never ready to take such cheek with resignation, the gods always retaliate by sending a nemesis that devastates such brass necks.

Even sadder is the brilliant young manager of enormous capability rising early to the top and then staying there for decades though every smidgen of originality has long since withered. These are the woodworm men: they look sound old oak beams that would support a mansion, but their strength has long been hollowed out and rotted away.

Conversely there are the slow starters who take a long time to find their feet, learn the ropes, and work out a modus vivendi with others. They need time to suss out the job, but impatient managers make the mistake of firing them before the investment has paid off.

Appraising the practical

All this applies to desk jobs only. In productive work the task is much more straightforward thanks to having something measurable, but more complicated due to having to set up piece rate and time and motion studies.[12]

This leaves wonderful opportunities for an individual with imagination. As Robert Townsend (former chairman of Avis car rental company) remarked 'The world seems to be divided into those who produce results

Alex PEATTIE + TAYLOR

BUT, ALEX, I THOUGHT WE WERE GOING TO SPEND THE WEEKEND PLANNING OUR CAREER STRATEGIES...

I KNOW, CLIVE...

BUT I HAPPENED TO PICK UP PENNY'S BOOK ON NEW AGE SPIRITUAL CONSCIOUSNESS. READING IT HAS MADE ME SEE RIGHT THROUGH THE SHALLOW EMPTINESS OF THE FINANCIAL WORLD.

I DON'T BELIEVE IT... LET ME SEE THAT...

"ONE MUST EMBARK ON AN INNER VOYAGE TO SELF-REALISATION IN ORDER TO GROW AND FIND ONE'S OWN PERSONAL SELF-WORTH"... BUT THIS IS JUST A LOAD OF VAPID PRETENTIOUS CLAPTRAP...

EXACTLY. AND IT'S WRITTEN IN ALMOST EXACTLY THE SAME LANGUAGE AS THIS EXECUTIVE RECRUITMENT MANUAL.

HOW TO BE HEAD-HUNTED

and those who get the credit'.[13] (See also **Promotion**, page 45, for how this helps with self-promotion.)

Tactics for executives Pre-empt judgements about your own performance by producing reports which are circulated to senior managers. These should be simple and replete with graphics and figures to give you a chance to be wonderfully creative with facts.

Take line graphs and histograms for instance. By adjusting the Y axis and not starting it at zero you can make even the slightest growth look startlingly huge; by making the axis logarithmic you can comprehensively distort comparisons. By using the word `average' as either the arithmetic mean or the median – occasionally both within a single set of figures – you can fake even more results.

The delightful thing about really distorting numbers is that everybody expects words to be slippery and unreliable but figures have a spuriously splendid air of accuracy.[14] Not only that but even if you happen to hit on someone unexpectedly sophisticated with statistics and he spots the legerdemain, you can plausibly disclaim any intention to deceive: they are just different presentations of the same figures, and you still believe yours to be the clearer.

29

Discipline

This is where the law stops ... and I start

The word discipline rouses some pretty alarming concepts in a few people. Some dream of a menacing Madame Whiplash in leathers and stilettos, or spanking parties in school uniforms. Working versions are less fun even than such physical pain, but enormous opportunities for manipulating the system.

Discipline in essence is motivating people to work the right way and slapping them down if they disagree. The right way is your way. Army sergeants have been coaching squaddies with this for ever: there are three ways of doing things – the right way, the wrong way and the army way. Here you will do things the army way. In the same way companies have to be nudged, coaxed and pummelled into your way of doing things. If you are shrewd that means not just getting the people below you to do brilliant and onerous work for which you can take the credit, but manipulating the boss to do something helpful for a change.

I Motivation

Producing motivation is one of the five major tasks of management,[1] the other four being:

- organising work
- communicating
- establishing measures of performance
- developing people

All work and no play makes Jack a dull boy

The first but probably the toughest challenge for a manager is to motivate not only subordinates but also superiors to help in his work and career because that, perplexingly enough, is sometimes not other people's primary aim in life. The shrewd operator therefore so corrals them that they help him when they think they are helping themselves.

For instance, private ambitions have only intermittent contact with the employer's objectives. There are admittedly some people for whom their work is life itself and they want nothing beyond it. Husbands, wives, children, and aged parents are ignored; hobbies are for schoolboys; and their only exercise is lifting a telephone. Spectacular successes admittedly come from the ranks of these obsessives who sleep four hours a day and labour mightily the other twenty.

If that dedication and effort are coupled with the sort of ingenuity and elaborate self-help set out in this book, and is aided by at least a tolerable level of ability, such people are hard to beat. Not impossible, for there are always really nasty unfair means, but difficult.

But for sensible people work is necessary pain to pay for pleasure. Sure, they like the social aspects of being at work, but their ambitions are to have nice holidays and comfortable houses.

Tactics for executives If you are one of those sensible people for whom work is the gap between fun and who has ambitions greater than becoming the best buying clerk in the company, you will realise that grabbing the attention of people at work is not easy and persuading them into a course of action is even harder. It takes stick and carrot, reward and punishment, positive and negative reinforcement – pick your own cliché.[2]

But precisely what reward, how is it to be administered and to whom? You know very well money is a help but it is not everything.[3]

Careful reading of the behavioural psychology texts produces some wonderfully successful ways of getting people to do what you want.

For instance, carefully chosen words of praise at precise timings will bend most of your staff to what you want more precisely than any rules or punishments. This is because reward has been experimentally found to be better at nudging people in the right direction than threats or punishments, and intermittent rewards the most effective of all. Isn't science wonderful?

The same schemes can be used on a boss as well. Remember, nobody is immune to well-administered stroking – it may be flattery, congratulations on an achievement, or a hint of having overheard his boss say how well something has been done. The exact method has to be adapted to the individual, but some form of approval will work with everybody. There is no curmudgeon so hardened that approval by colleagues does not feel better than hatred or distaste. Having found the lever, you pull it to shunt the train onto your siding. It could be used for something as nebulous as getting the boss to think well of you.

There are other more immediate means as well. One of them is the old body language cliché. Let us assume you want to promote some devious scheme that needs the boss's approval. Every time the boss discusses the scheme or even touches on a related topic show interest and approval: lean forward in your chair to show attention, look eager, perhaps even smile. Every time he drifts away to something else lean back, glance down at your notes, cross your legs, and look bored. It will be surprising how often the topic will drift back to the subject you want to discuss.

The same sort of technique can be used to ditch a colleague by means so subtle nothing can ever be pinned on you. Carefully placed disparagement in tone rather than content, apparent apathy and boredom when the person or subject comes up, and carefully worded praise so faint as to be inaudible, will all work their magic. 'I tried to tell him your idea was really innovative', you will be able to say in all transparent honesty.

As for motivating the workforce under you, that requires a few of the strategies for dealing with bosses, but it needs a more direct and complex set of encouragement and manipulation. One great trick is not to assume everybody is like yourself and motivated by the same preferences. Watch them carefully to find their weaknesses and needs. What reward you use depends on what people need. Remember George Bernard Shaw's dictum 'Do not do unto others as you would they should do unto you. Their tastes may not be the same'.[4]

The basic minimum is to get in place the so-called hygiene[5] factors without which people start getting disgruntled and obstructive. These are the fundamentals like minimum acceptable working conditions, adequate salary and an apparent job security. Note those adjectives – they are significant. You really do not have to go over the top with even hygiene factors.

The point about these is that if they are absent employees are miserable but their presence merely removes the grounds for hostility. Actually to make people happy it is not enough to remove grounds that irk them, it needs an altogether different set of factors, like achievement, recognition, responsibility and progress.

In other words hygiene factors to prevent active disruption are mainly physical needs that can be unloaded onto somebody else, so if they go

33

wrong and the company is faced with strikes or absenteeism it is nothing to do with you. Indeed, you can get remarkable loyalty from staff by appearing to stand up against Them in trying to extract better working conditions.

On the other hand, rewards that nudge people into working harder and longer than their contract requires are psychological and under your own control. There are still sceptics who see staff as forms of galley slaves, to be lashed whenever they raise their heads, and for a time even that can work. But not for long. The more devious means work better and longer. But you do not have to be a psychology graduate or a fervent believer in all the theory to use the techniques.

All the same, it is best to be wary of management fads. They come and go with increasing frequency. Japanese management has continued to be fashionable despite the obvious trauma of the Japanese economy, suggesting their companies beat Western counterparts because instead of command structures they have shared values and consult widely.[6]

Attempts to replicate the system in the West have failed because the theory conveniently overlooked that the system is driven by two factors unique to Japan. Firstly, a company is reckoned to do an enormous favour in providing employment and the individual is morally bound to uphold his honour by reciprocating with devoted effort. Secondly, the Japanese consult widely not because they deem it democratically suitable but because it is a cause of profound shame to fail or make a serious error in one's own area of expertise. If, however, the decision cannot be attributed to an individual but to a consensus, if something goes wrong no one person is to blame.

It's time to kick ass

When an unpopular decision has to be made or when the outcome is liable to be dodgy, make sure there is widespread discussion, consultation and agreement. That way a disaster can be easily deflected onto somebody convenient.

II Reprimands and warnings

For all your best attempts to have people do what you want, sometimes they fail or become recalcitrant. Then there really is nothing for it but to knock them into line. The question is for what, when, and how.

The first important rule to remember is not to slap people down for making mistakes. 'The man who makes no mistakes does not usually make anything', wisely remarked Bishop Magee.[7] If you want people to use their initiative, to improve on what is being done now and to branch out into new work, they have to be given the chance to take a risk.

Intelligent people learn from others' mistakes, but if you are venturing out with a bit of imagination into dangerously new territory, there is no safe path. What is inexcusable is not an error, but stupidity and carelessness. If even brief thought or a bit of application would have sufficed to avoid an expensive bump, then doubts are justified and a repetition merits a reprimand.

Deserving of a rap across the knuckles, or even a legally required warning which is the prelude to the boot, is failing to do the job properly (see **Performance**, page 17), or all the silly and unpleasant things for which you can justifiably sack somebody (see next chapter).

In addition there are also the lesser misdemeanours for which you need only put a shot across the bows. These are the inconveniences which make

I've got a head for business and a body for sin

life for others difficult. For instance, lust may be a sin but only becomes a business problem when it shows up as an indiscreet or careless extramarital affair. These take managers' minds off the work, leave them open to anything from awkwardness to blackmail, and often put a worrying strain on their finances.

If the affair is with someone in the same company the problem is squared. Actually, sex with somebody in the same company is pretty stupid even if both are single – it is merely a distraction when things go well, but a serious disruption when the affair breaks up.

Putting a stop to that sort of nonsense is easy. You use precisely the blackmail against which you are warning the incompetent adulterer, without of course saying anything explicit. That can be even more effective when applied upwards. Catch the boss at it on the office couch, or even just in mid-grope and there is no end to the long advantage to be gained, so long as you do not push your luck.

But it is just as well to remember that the best sort of discipline is not aimed at some sort of revenge and punishment, but at achieving your end. One of the ends is to get the business working better.

The problem arises when someone is not doing well. Possible solutions can be more encouragement or training, the setting of more realistic targets, or simply reallocating the person to a job more suited to the individual's talents and preferences. An illustration of this was when Frederick the Great, riding through the camp of his favourite cavalry regiment, saw a man about to be executed. Why are you doing that, he protested, he is one of my best soldiers. Because, came the reply, he has been buggering the horses. Don't be silly, said the king, that is no reason to kill him and waste a good soldier – put him in the infantry.

Happiness is a warm gun

Tactics for executives Make friends with the secretaries not just of the top people but throughout the organisation – they always know what is going on.

That way you can find out about people's social, sexual, and employment difficulties. For your own subordinates this enables you to anticipate difficulties and counter them with warnings, changes of responsibilities, or preventive measures. Against bosses such information provides useful ammunition.

III Sacking

Sooner or later the ultimate disciplinary sanction will be necessary and someone will have to be sacked (for redundancies see **Staff turnover**). Be very wary, and preferably get somebody else to do the dirty work.

Tactics for executives There are two reasons for handing the task to someone else. Firstly, unless you want to strike terror into the hearts of your subordinates (and there are times when that is useful) it is just as well for someone else to get the odium of kicking somebody out onto the street.

If you have, however, just arrived at a new department which seems dozy and inept and you want to wake it up with a brutal kick to the groin there is nothing more effective than a couple of loud and vituperative sackings.

The second, and more important, reason for getting somebody else to take over the chore is because it is a legal minefield. Step just one inch off the narrow path and you could get your wallet blown off.

Even if you are a hundred and twenty-three per cent right to get rid of that person, be sure of both the grounds and the procedure, and prepare with elaborate care. There are some fifty thousand applications a year to

the industrial tribunals alleging a sacking has been unfair or the employer has failed to follow the Industrial Relations Act 1971 and the Employment Protection (Consolidation) Act 1978.

Wrongful dismissal is defined as failure to give proper notice or being unjustifiably peremptory in sacking someone. Far more common is the allegation of unfair dismissal. To be recognised as fair the employer has to show he acted reasonably and the employee was dismissed due to one of the following:

- lack of ability
- misconduct
- redundancy
- legal problems

Ability

If an employee is not performing it is only fair (quite apart from the legal requirements) to say what the problem is and how and by when the work must improve. The law provides some exceptions to this. One is where such skill is necessary that a single failure is a justification for getting shot of them. For instance a pilot whose landing was so bumpy the plane was damaged was allowed to be dismissed out of hand.[9]

Senior executives are also excepted from preliminary warnings because they should know what is needed and whether they are providing it.

A third category where there is little point in prolonging the agony is where 'the inadequacy of performance is so extreme that there must be an irredeemable incapability'.[10] But do not rely on this as it does not succeed often.

Being too ill to continue the work is also taken as lack of capability.

Misconduct

Misconduct is itself a charmingly vague term. The legal establishment has

always claimed such diffuse wording enables courts to enforce common sense, whereas exact and logical explicitness can lead to manifest nonsense. It is perhaps fortunate then for lawyers that such imprecision requires innumerable cases to be fought to define the boundaries. And so it is here. A growing volume of case law has produced a range of headings which may be a help including:

- disobedience
- absence
- insubordination
- crime

Even absence, apparently the most obvious and clear of these, is less straightforward than at first it seems. Persistent lateness is grounds, but only after at least one warning, and for absence to be the reason it has to be 'insupportable' and the employer has to have regard to previous record. On the other hand being continually ill is an acceptable reason for giving someone the sack, according to the law.[11]

Drunkenness, not unreasonably, counts as misconduct but falling down on the job once is not grounds for the sack – except, again, for airline pilots. But if after at least two warnings the employee continues to turn up zonked even the law permits the heave-ho.

There is surprisingly little case law on bribery. It is best to be safe, however, and avoid becoming the great legal precedent. One way to do this is to set out for staff where the limits lie. Some managers take a nice simple view: friendship with suppliers and customers is fine, but presents are unacceptable. Mostly the line is a little more pragmatic than that: a bottle of Scotch at Christmas is all right, but a case of Château Petrus 1966 is over the top; a box of chocs is dandy, a holiday in Bermuda is not.

It is hard to define the limits though. One manager offered his staff this guidance: 'Just think what it would look like if published in *Private Eye*'. On the other hand one journalist used to have a more self-assured and comfortable line: 'I can't be bought, but please don't stop trying'.

Insubordination is hard to prove. Dumb insolence is not enough, nor is calling the manager a stupid punk after five years' good service.[12] What you can say, it seems, depends on who is speaking to whom – the same words from a foreman to a worker have different connotations when coming from an employee talking to a boss.

According to *Modern Employment Law* by M. Winchup,[13] 'there have been half a dozen cases on the precise meaning of "fuck off" – apparently a common industrial salutation'. It seems that when a supervisor uses the words the meaning can range from a 'general exhortation'[14] to a demotion.[15]

Redundancy
See **Staff turnover.**

The law
The legal problem is the easiest to dispose of. For instance, a lorry driver with his licence snatched by a magistrate is useless and can be replaced without too many legal hazards.

IV Grievance

The converse of the managerial reprimand is cause for employee objection. These are the grievances that can be about tangible, physical things like the

It's important to be nice, but nicer to be important

loos lacking paper, or there being not enough parking places. Partially physical, with psychological overtones, are things like repetitive strain injury which can cause paralysis of an arm. Then there are the subjective problems, often hopes and fears, which are the ones that take up most time.[16]

Before anything sensible can be done about complaints you have to disentangle what the worker claims to be the problem and the pretext for the complaint, from the underlying worry which even the worker may not have consciously recognised.[17]

Workers too insecure to complain or whose grievances have been rejected in a cavalier fashion can become increasingly cheesed off, and that can result in anything from apathy to arson.[18] If there are large numbers of such disgruntled people the result can be sabotage or strikes.

Tactics for executives For an executive expecting to be disciplined or even sacked, there are several ploys to sidestep nemesis. But whatever you do needs to be swift and decisive, so you had better have the plans ready long before disaster actually strikes. Alternatively, you can take avoiding action.

One way is to become indispensable. Say you are an accountant in the finance department who sees the finance manager closing in for a kill. There is little point in becoming good at the job. It is too late for that and besides that never was a criterion for success (see **Promotion**). No, the answer is to draw up a plan for saving the organisation a fortune.

It should be complex enough to be impressive and require at least nine pages to explain, but simple enough for a director to understand. Take this not to your boss – that is where the danger lies – but to the finance director or even straight to the managing director.

41

The best way to help the poor is not to become one of them

Similarly, salesmen and sales managers can work out cheaper ways to allocate resources, reduce staff or increase turnover by reassigning areas or lines; production people can show more effective streams through the plant; and so on.

Needless to say it will take some time to implement, and the details of putting the plan in place had to be omitted from your document for the sake of brevity. In fact the plan may not just gain you a reprieve – it could pave the path to promotion.

There is one other important factor to watch out for: the scapegoat. When the sky falls in, profits crash, a product fails, the unions walk out, or the share price plunges, someone must be at fault. It is unlikely the chairman or chief executive will appear in Cheapside in sackcloth loudly wailing *mea culpa, mea maxima culpa* and flogging themselves with studded whips, having collected their P45s on the way. No. A slightly more common reaction is: `What sir? me sir? no sir, him sir'. So if you see disaster about to happen, step out from under.

Actually, if handled well, getting the sack does not have to be a disaster at all. If word gets around you left because of a difference of opinion with an intransigent and incompetent chairman, offers of directorships could well flow in, and you could always make a name as a company doctor.

Here is how to get all of those things. Preparation starts from the moment you are contemplating joining the company. As soon as the company looks keen to hire you, the sensible candidate will hold out for a careful contract containing provisions for a golden handshake and golden parachute.

This is why you can read every day in the papers about the departure of some director who is sacked for intemperate negligence, arrogant stupidity,

or Olympic class incompetence, yet despite having lost his company millions he is given 'compensation for loss of office' running to hundreds of thousands of pounds. That director had a good contract.

A word of warning: be sure you really do want to be bound tightly. Not long ago a well-known executive was prepared to join an organisation notorious for its revolving door for senior people only if the famous legal firm of Goodman Derrick drew up a watertight employment contract. He was much chagrined when eighteen months later it was discovered the lawyers had done their work too well and he couldn't leave for a far better job.

It is worth noting that for an organisation such contracts are an admission of failure. Since when was motivation or loyalty guaranteed by a scrap of paper? If a good manager will not stay because the work is fun and the pay is good, it seems unlikely that being manacled to a desk will much improve performance. Contracts are a way for nervous directors to ensure predictable departure is cushioned by cash.

Assuming such contracts are not available, acceptable or felt necessary, it is worth having some negotiating ploys available when the Dear John interview does come around and it becomes necessary to dodge doom.

If you do not have exquisite grounds for wrongful or unfair dismissal, departure needs rat-like cunning to extract an unfair deal from the about-to-be ex-employer. Given self-control and self-possession the departing manager has some surprisingly large psychological advantages:

- most people feel uncomfortable about kicking someone out even if they have richly deserved it
- everybody dislikes painful and ugly scenes and can therefore be embarrassed while the departing person has absolutely nothing to lose

- for similar reasons it is possible to prevent the sacker gaining the high moral ground by ignoring catalogues of misdeeds with contempt
- and rejecting all attempts to induce deference
- directors can be made to feel small-minded and niggardly with surprising ease

Hasta la vista, baby The departure itself will be eased and the interview given a certain edge if you have the self-confidence born of alternative survival. The fast-moving and shrewd survivor has always got a plan for contingencies. That applies to careers as well. Any sensible executive will have another iron in the fire even if it is still tepid. Whether occasional journalism, casual consultancy, investment in a restaurant, non-executive directorship of a small business, there should be something there to provide a base and an income.

An alternative will provide you with the confidence to play the game to the limit, knowing you have nothing to lose. Some useful hints for the departure negotiations are:

- always mention from the beginning that any agreement is subject to discussion with your lawyers
- hint at the preparation of a company profile for the *Daily Telegraph* or the *Financial Times*
- mention that the company car is not for work at all but part of the remuneration package and can therefore not be reclaimed
- insist on other non-monetary perks (easier to negotiate because they will not show in the annual accounts)
- point out that pension payments by the company are to continue until you move into another job or retire [19]

44

Promotion

Power is the ultimate aphrodisiac

1 Power

'Power is the ultimate aphrodisiac' said Henry Kissinger,[1] who became a well-known `swinger' on his short illusion of having some. If you are not in business for power, money and sex what is all the labour and striving for? Many people will say they work for money but in fact they put in such gruelling hours the cash is usually spent by their divorced spouses. They want the power and control senior jobs carry. That is a strong motivator.

It goes without saying, therefore, that the best way to ensure loyalty, enthusiasm and effort is by rewarding people, and the best reward is promotion. But wait a moment. Things that go without saying generally stop when said. For instance, take a more careful look at that dictum about promotion. The first reaction is to say `Of course'. Once you stop to think about how the real world operates the reaction changes to `Yes, but'.

On the other hand it really *does* go without saying in many of the major textbooks on personnel management the subject is so far from being discussed in them that the word is absent even from the index.

When it comes to using promotion – both your own and that of the people below you – there is little established help on the tactics of advantage. Yet for a manager there are only three carrots to persuade people to work harder than is reasonable: praise and appreciation, pay increases, and promotion. But the greatest of these is promotion: it provides the pay rise automatically, and greater praise scarcely exists.

| Alex | PEATTIE + TAYLOR | TELL YOU THE TRUTH, ALEX: I SPEND MY WEEKENDS JUST LIKE ANY OTHER HUSBAND AND FATHER OF TWO... | SATURDAY MORNINGS, THE WIFE AND I GO SHOPPING FOR THE WEEKLY GROCERIES DOWN AT THE LOCAL SUPERMARKET.. | AND AS A MATTER OF FACT IT'S A LOT OF FUN. WE BOTH ENJOY IT. | WHO PUSHES THE TROLLEY? / THE CHAUFFEUR. |

You're quite a little soldier: consider this a military funeral

Tactics for executives It follows therefore that the doing of it and the promise of it are powerful weapons in the hands of an astute executive. The most effective form of loyalty is the one that follows self-interest. Make clear your role in the promotion battles and your subordinates will support you to distraction.

This permits a range of devious ploys. For instance, there is the thrusting, aggressive, and dangerously able youngster clearly angling for at least your job. Given the possession also of even a minimal shrewdness and organisational manoeuvring, such people rise through companies with remorseless glee. Assuming you cannot divert them to other careers or companies and there is no obvious shrewd shot that will sink the aspirant for ever, the answer is to use their energy to your own advantage.

The first move is to block access to the people above except through you. Since one of the ways of leapfrogging up the organisation is to circumvent one's own boss, managers must block such links. This has not only the negative function of preventing the slimy toads below from pulling a fast one by using your own techniques, but has the positive advantage of perforce making you the object of their loyalty.

Make clear to the thruster that personal progress depends on outstanding performance in the present job on your assessment. That will unleash such energy that others in the department will be shamed into trying harder as well. This has the rather pleasant incidental advantage of making you seem super-efficient as your section produces miracles of output. But it also means the young thruster will eventually have to be rewarded.

When promotion can no longer be reasonably delayed, place the person very carefully. That does not mean in a tough job or facing a notorious

46

challenge, because there is just a chance that the bounder might find some wonderful solution to an intractable problem or at least the semblance of it. Far better to relegate such dangerous people to important-sounding titles in obscure backwaters of worthy but dreary monotony, away from head office.

II The company's benefit

For the company itself, promoting people through the organisation rather than recruiting for a vacancy from outside has some spectacular advantages:

- it shows management notices and cares
- it provides encouragement to effort
- there is no cost in finding and selecting
- training and induction costs are avoided

But promotion is not quite that wonderful – there is a cost to everything. If something seems too good to be true, it usually is. And so it is in this case. Even for the best-organised company internal promotion is fraught with peril and has several drawbacks:

- a good performer at existing levels (say a good salesman) is lost to the company
- being good at one job (eg. selling) does not guarantee performance one level up (as, say, sales manager)
- loyal service is not of itself evidence of competence
- beware the 'halo' effect
- steady promotion incurs the risks of the Peter Principle: 'in a hierarchy

every employee tends to rise to his level of incompetence'[2]

- disaffection in the ranks: 'Every time I fill a vacancy I create a hundred malcontents and one ingrate', Louis XIV discovered

Trust me, he'll live

Operators as managers

Losing a sound operator through promotion is a classic sign of a manager who lets a soft heart rule a soft head. One feels an instinctive sympathy with somebody who has done well for years and believes they have earned a handsome reward. So they may, but not necessarily promotion. Give them a bonus, a company car, an extra week's holiday, buy their discontent off with a matching pen and pencil set, a plaque to hang on the wall, or a lavish dinner. But unless they are really likely to be good one level up for heaven's sake do not promote them.

The normal response to that advice is that the person will leave and might go to a competitor. So what? If they are entering at the same level it shows only that the other company is paying better, which can easily be rectified. If it is on promotion, it serves the silly people right.

On the other hand dogmatism leads to predictable failure. Flexibility (usually a euphemism for indecision) can have surprising benefits. Occasionally there is a middle manager who is doing good work and is desperately keen for promotion, but you are undecided. They are admittedly doing well in the organisation and might even have some of the qualities for promotion but just seem to lack the stature, air of command or the real sense of position and gravitas for the next job up. If they really are keen to rise, it is sometimes worth giving them a bash at it. For one thing it will improve internal morale (except for the rivals to the job), few will know better how to keep a check on the

people in the next level down, and (most importantly) it is amazing how people grow into a job.

As the old proverb has it, God gives broad shoulders when He gives the heavy burdens.

Leadership

Come with me if you want to live

'What we want is great leadership', is the permanent cry. Hundreds of studies have tried to identify the ingredients of successful leaders, but have failed to find a formula. All they found was that people generally agreed to have leadership qualities (whatever those are) also had some of the following qualities:

- above average intelligence
- ability to solve abstract problems
- independence/inventiveness/ imagination (qualities which decline after the age of forty)
- energy to take action swiftly
- self–assurance
- ability to take a broader view
- unusual height
- health
- upper middle or upper class back-ground[3]

Needless to say paragons who have all these qualities do not exist, and the factors needed for effective leadership are present in only about two per cent of the population, irrespective of education, training or any other aid.

The notion that this sort of talent can be acquired is romantic twaddle. The tacit assumption is that if we merely dedicate ourselves and acquire some new mechanical skills we can become anything we want. In fact, all real achievement requires the sort of application that would be considered neurotic in any other context. If, as Edison said, 'genius is one per cent

inspiration and ninety-nine per cent perspiration',[4] just think how much perspiration is needed by the merely talented but dogged.

The point is that if you have an aptitude for painting, an art school can help supply technique; a musical skill can be enhanced by advice and practice; and even athletic prowess can be maximised by clever training. In the absence of any innate ability such tuition can at least prevent you looking an absolute prat, but little more.

Do not despair. With application and guidance most of us can do a lot better than we imagine and even outdo the untutored natural. Even the much-vaunted charisma can be acquired since it is little more than enthusiasm, determination and effective communication.[5]

One sign of a bad boss – and hence a poor leader (therefore unsuited for further promotion) – is the constitutional inability to delegate. It is often a sign of insecurity that he hugs the work to himself or continuously breathes down the neck of his subordinates. If it is really true, as many of these people proclaim, that if you want something done you have to do it yourself, then their recruiting policies have been disastrous.

Loyalty

Loyalty should be rewarded. More to the point, it must be seen to be rewarded. One answer is a system of carefully graded rewards and privileges – a sort of honours system. Shell for instance has a series of lapel badges with the colour of an inset stone indicating the length of service. Some companies organise entertainments graded to time, seniority and performance, some provide presents like wall plates or carriage clocks, some have special clubs, most make a mention of long-serving people in the house magazine.

The 'halo' effect

Managers are wonderfully prone to provide sweeping generalisations from a statistical sample of one: a woman manager did very well in the Leeds office so women make good managers; women are right for Leeds, and so on. This is similar to the 'halo' effect: Fred made a good sales manager so he will be a good production manager.

In any case the assessment of people is notoriously fallible (see **Recruitment**, page 2) whether for promotion or anything else.

Most managers try to create in their own image. This is (often) not from a self-serving conceit but a predictable preference shared by the rest of the population for people like ourselves, partly because we like what we understand. It is this rather than rampant prejudice that has ensured white middle-class men are most likely to be promoted.

There is still suspicion of people with regional accents: Londoners think anything north of Watford is rough and alien, and northerners are prone to think the south is full of soft snobs. With such universal wariness generalised into xenophobia some groups have problems. European immigrants can assimilate quite quickly and become invisible, but it is tougher for a Pakistani, a Jamaican, or a woman to pass unnoticed as white middle-class Englishmen.

The Peter Principle

The problem for any organisation is not just finding the bright young people and keeping them with promises of rewards (including promotion), but also of chopping out the dead wood to give these green young shoots room to flourish. Top managers have not only generally risen to their level of incompetence, but all too easily have lapsed into a routine, and become

isolated from the rest of the company. They listen only to sycophants and PR men, ignore the rampant bureaucracy and confusion growing around them, and think they are walking on water when in fact they are treading on the submerged bodies of busy workers.

Experience is generally just a euphemism for impotent old age. Few can maintain the energy generated by tackling a new problem and hardly any keep the freshness of mind to go on questioning accepted practice after five years.

If after that initial burst of creativity and thrust they are not ready to be promoted further it is as well to shift them into a different area to try and keep the momentum going by presenting new challenges. The great danger is of people rising swiftly to positions of power just as they run out of ideas and energy. It is so common as to become almost a cliché.

There is a long tradition of regicide over much of the primitive world in areas where qualities of leadership are essential for the prosperity or even survival of a group. As a leader's abilities decline a convenient removal is arranged.[6] Similar principles for similar reasons are appropriate to senior managers and, a fortiori, to chief executives.

Disaffection

If two people are competing for an internal promotion the loser is bound to be disaffected. He may grow disgruntled and uncooperative. A certain amount of sulking is excusable but you must take care it does not curdle into subversiveness, and you may not want the person to leave.

One way to placate the loser is to provide compensation. That can involve a pay rise, but the employee will realise he is just being bought off

and it may increase his resentment. A better ploy is to provide balm for a bruised ego: give the person a project, a challenge that will make them feel wanted, shows you trust and value them, and takes their minds off the disappointment. Obviously it has to be a real task or the person will be even less gruntled if given a nonsense job.

Tactics for senior managers If you happen to be chairman or whatever, and you begin to spot ambitious young managers and directors sharpening their sacrificial daggers, there are really three options:

- find new reserves of creative boost
- pull up the drawbridge and fight off the usurpers
- fill your pockets from the corporate coffers and then leave gracefully

The first of these is the hardest in practice. Some people need the stimulus of danger or pressure to mobilise frenetic activity and can summon a torrent of ideas and imagination in their seventies or even eighties, plus the energy to see them into application. Churchill is often cited in this context by optimistic old men, having become prime minister for the first time at the age of sixty-six and for the second time at seventy-seven. But such people are rare and even Churchill was gaga near the end of his second term.

Where age really tells is in the hard-earned scars of corporate battles and the consequent knowledge of wily tactics and elaborate experience of organisational in-fighting. Those will help defeat for a long time all but the most concerted and expert attempts at regicide.

If you have no stomach for such a struggle or reckon it is futile and demeaning, the best tactic is to hint that you will fight a long and

53

internecine war to maintain your power base unless attractive terms can make departure more enticing. This is made even more of a powerful position by holding some of the company's shares. Such an approach is called blackmail and usually works. It will be all the more effective if the other side is convinced by your make-my-day determination, as well as by the reassurance it is not just paying Danegeld and you really will go away given the right incentive.

The package finally accepted will depend on the departing manager's personal preferences but should usually include a big boost to the salary prior to departure to bump up the pension entitlement, an additional golden handshake as an ex-gratia payment, and sometimes a continuing source of income in the form of 'consultancy'.

Tactics for executives Whatever management schools and textbooks say, the people who prosper in large organisations understand not the business but the structure. It is the ones who know when not to bother with actually doing the work but to concentrate on taking credit for it; the ones who pick their friends and moments; the ones who manage artfully to back into the limelight; and the ones who know not just their boss's problems and motivations but also his superiors; these are the ones who rise rapidly up the system. They know the primary rule for promotion and indeed all corporate success: working no substitute for effective politics.[7]

There are people who profess a lofty disdain for corporate in-fighting. There are some who claim to be too nice to indulge in devious, vicious and time-consuming manoeuvring. And there still remain a few who believe such conduct is unnecessary.

Let him who desires peace prepare for war

This is an admirable stance of selfless dedication, but suitable only for those happy to remain at the bottom of the structure and resigned to seeing credit for their work being taken by someone else. They should also be immune to annoyance when shafted by their more ambitious colleagues. This book is not for them.

For the rest of us such idealistic detachment from the realities of corporate behaviour seems admirable if naive. Such charmingly unrealistic people are seldom a threat and should therefore be used rather than fought. As for the rest, you need a two-fold policy:

- one positive, to gain advantage
- one negative or defensive, to prevent competitors winning at your expense

The shrewd opportunist is ready for change that is about to happen. Being ready is so much more than half the battle that what precisely you are ready for is almost beside the point. The wide range of strategies available for being the obvious person to promote requires the flexible response. The policies can be grouped under four main headings:

- knowing how to take credit
- visibility
- wrong–footing your boss
- mobility

Taking credit
Renown has nothing to do with achievement and everything to do with shrewd public relations.[8] For instance, there are Columbus day parades in New York though he never got beyond Cuba and the continent is named

after Amerigo Vespucci who set foot on the mainland in 1499. But what about Leif Ericsson who in AD 970 landed in Massachusetts or Labrador, or even Cabot who landed in Newfoundland in 1497? The point is that getting there first is not the same as getting the credit. The two require different abilities.

You have only to look at the charmingly ambiguous meaning the phrase 'taking credit' to realise how deeply embedded the concept is in our psyche. Credit can be in the form of praise and fame, or in the sense of money. As Ogden Nash pointed out when explaining the continent had been named after someone most people now have never heard of:

> So the sad fate of Columbus ought to be pointed out to
>   every child and voter
> Because it has a very important moral, which is, Don't be a
>   discoverer, be a promoter.

If there is credit in the monetary sense you are on a different tack. Here we are concerned with garnering any praise going and riding it like a surfboard to promotion, better jobs and higher salaries.

In this sense, however, taking credit is a more subtle procedure than merely elbowing your way to the front and bellowing 'It's me, I did it'. For one thing any factual statement that is disprovable should be avoided; for another, people have an instinctive wariness of braggadocio. There are places in the world where overt and sustained self-promotion is considered sound and acceptable behaviour, and a welcome sign of confidence.

Britons trust only justified modesty. What they really like is agreeable mediocrity and only if that is unavailable will they accept brain and energy,

but on condition that such talents are elaborately disguised behind a facade of bumbling humility. Fortunately there is always a ready supply of unassuming inadequates.

This means you cannot afford to be too brazen in showing your cleverness – itself a term of abuse only in England. So when something appears to be going right you start laying the foundations by dropping hints about how hard you are working to avoid a potential disaster. In other words, build up the complexity, difficulty and danger of the task to make victory that much more laudable, and at the same time subtly emphasise your own pivotal function.

When success is finally apparent ensure everybody knows about it, but subtly. Shuffle disarmingly into the limelight with deprecating mumbles of 'Just doing my job' 'It was hard work but of course we were jolly lucky' 'I had a good team to help me' 'I do hope people will not expect this every day.'

The trick is, as you will have spotted, to praise by faint damns.

Visibility
One course to success has always been visibility. Being seen around the company, meeting senior managers is part of it. It gets your name known and, given the right impression, a director may just remember the bright young executive the next time there is a vacancy.

In addition, you do not have to be a Lee Iacocca, John Harvey-Jones, John Scully, or Harold Geneen to pontificate on business; no rule says middle managers, for instance, should not publish. They can go the academically respectable route of serious studies in heavy journals, or they can aim for such shallow and unsatisfactory goals as fame and riches. The latter is easier.

All it takes is a new slogan, but one so simple it can be immediately understood. Its truth is irrelevant. Indeed any notion that can be encapsulated in words every chairman can understand in fifteen seconds cannot possibly be true.

For instance, Douglas McGregor grew famous on the rule that there are two types of management: Theory X which is authoritarian, and Theory Y which is participative.[9] It takes but a moment's thought to realise that only on a management school blackboard is life that clear.

The idea does not have to be original, nor even particularly right, and it should not be too clever; it must be easy to propound and package, and sound sufficiently plausible that distraught managers will try to implement its teachings.

Even if enormous fame eludes you, there are ways of gaining greater exposure than would be justified by mere rank or even talent. Get to know journalists and feed them scraps of information: not necessarily about your own company – gossip and scurrilous rumours about others will be just as welcome. When they come to accept your expertise on an industry they will ring you up for comment they can quote. From there it is merely a matter of being available to pontificate with pungent concision and journalists will adore you and give you more publicity than you can cope with.

There is a danger in this. It will raise envy and resentment in the rest of the organisation unless you are so senior your right to be a spokesman cannot be gainsaid. The first time your name appears in print may require justification. If necessary lie shamelessly: you never spoke to the journalist; you never discussed those matters; you never said any of the things quoted; you insisted anything said was off the record or unattributable. Journalists

will not grass on you no matter how much you traduce them, being too concerned to be known to hold on to contacts and keep them happy. Besides, they get it all the time.

If the public relations manager protests it is his job to talk to the press you might suggest that if he had been doing it the hacks would not have come to you, and in any case is it not the job of PR to help communications rather than getting in the way?

Elimination

One route to promotion is the elimination of managers one level up. This is often made easier by the people concerned being senescent – an affliction which sets in remarkably early. Some executives start showing symptoms of Pick's disease surprisingly young. This is a pre-senile dementia of middle age which is characterised by 'personality disintegration, confusion, deterioration of intellectual capacity and function, impairment of memory and judgement'. Sound familiar?

Such people are intransigent and awkward, but they can readily be goaded by subtle picking at paranoias or prejudices until they burst a gasket. Preferably in public.

If they are still relatively alert, one ploy is to isolate or circumvent them. Initiate action that should rightly have come from your boss and write letters (especially to important people) which should in all conscience have been signed by him. Talk directly to his superiors at every need for a higher decision you are reluctant to take on your own. Pretty soon they will begin to wonder whether such an executive function is still needed and even if so whether you might not be more suitable for the post.

Yet another route is out and out assassination. This has its own set of complex rules. The first is: never make an open attack unless you are certain of winning quickly. There is no point in inviting bruising retaliation and hostility, and prolonged acrimonious struggles can do nothing but damage even if you eventually emerge the victor.

The second is in effect a by-product of the first: choose your moment to strike carefully. It is, for instance, so much easier and less effort to kick a man when he is down, and backs present a much larger and easier target for a dagger.

The third requirement for successful assassination is careful research: find out about the boss's weaknesses. Everybody has something murky or unsavoury hidden in their past, whether it concerns sex, drink, drugs, peculation or whatever.

Another way to help promotion is by foreign travel. Not by you but by your boss. Not only are such absences useful times for machinations, plots and general mischief, but prolonged and frequent thudding across the time zones makes most people irritable, inefficient, slower and distressed for up to a week afterwards. It probably also shortens life. So invent indispensable business trips.

Mobility

A streak of ruthlessness is also useful. Noël Coward used to say he always travelled by Italian ships because there was none of that damn nonsense about women and children first. In just the same way, winners are first to the ladder and have sufficiently pointed elbows to prevent anyone overtaking.

The most important characteristic of success is nimbleness. Stay long

In war there is no substitute for victory

enough in a job to benefit from the fruits of your predecessor's efforts and then move on in time for your successor to get the blame for what you have wrought. When you have run out of places to go you can always become a company doctor or a television pundit telling others how to do their jobs.

Other rewards
People talk about promotion as if it were just about titles. Forget about that – what matters is power and money. And those frequently have nothing to do with the public parade.

Take power for instance. The way ministers strut around Westminster you really would think they had the power to do more than just make asinine public statements. In fact, since they are seldom more than eighteen months in any job they are just beginning to understand its language before being shunted off to Agriculture or Employment or (if they have really irritated the prime minister) Northern Ireland.

So the ambitious manager may want to be chief executive, but only one person will get there. For the rest it is a choice of settling another rung lower down or moving sideways to money and influence.

Training

I coulda been a contender

Training is for footballers. In business it is for lathe operators and the like. That is the general view of most companies. Despite that most take the view that even shop–floor training is not worth the effort (and British footballers are not doing startlingly well).

Anybody bothering to plan for the medium term (ie. beyond tea-time tomorrow) will spot this as a bungalow argument – it has one flaw. It ignores a few minor problems like the continuing need for not only technically competent factory hands and fitters, but also capable sales and purchasing staff, competent accountancy people, managers with some knowledge of the business world and, heaven help us, top executives with a competence for the job.

There is admittedly the danger that managers will attempt to hide the errors of their recruiting by trying vainly to improve inadequate staff by stuffing technique into them. A vain effort, since geese stuffed with the wisdom of all the world still remain geese.

Tactics for executives If you have recruited a complete duffer, a well-meaning but blundering incompetent, you have a problem. Clearly you cannot afford passengers, but firing the individual entails admitting your inept selection and could provoke complex legal arguments (see **Discipline**, page 30). So you either palm him off onto another department, if necessary on promotion, or send him as far away as possible, for example on a

training course. It may seem a temporary solution, but it usually produces a range of solutions on the employee's return.

I The need for training

The need for training is fairly varied. For instance it includes:

- technical expertise for production staff
- specialist qualifications for professionals (eg. accountants, solicitors)
- MBAs
- physical training
- management training
- preparation for top management succession

Production
At the production level it is all relatively straightforward. Shop-floor training not only increases skills but makes employees more satisfied;[1] they feel they are making more of their potential and are on the road to higher earnings. Unhappily this is too vague a concept to make the investment seem sound to most boards of directors.[2]

The major problem for most companies is keeping the people they have trained. Other companies without the capital investment in education can afford to pay more to lure away the choice employees.

Where the effects of training are most clearly evident it should be least necessary as employees should have had such elementary knowledge and skills before joining. Typing and shorthand speeds and accuracy are easy to measure for instance, as is the output of a lathe operator, but hiring people without that sort of elementary competence is silly.

Professional qualifications

Most large companies have on board some specialist professionals, the most common being an accountant, occasionally as finance director. Sometimes there is also a lawyer, and so on.

The problem is that these specialists are closeted with their own narrow expertise, pontificating with growing authority as they become more expert and hence further and further from the comprehension of the rest of the organisation.

This is the sort of circumstance in which financial experts recommend policies of exemplary logic and sense – the only problem is that production, marketing, customers, distribution etc, fail to comply with their neat and orderly systems. The company then ploughs into the ground with the most elegant of plans understood very clearly by the specialists and the banks, and nobody else.

One way to counteract this insularity is to get the experts' fingernails dirty – keep retraining them. Second them from time to time to other sections and perhaps even make them talk to customers. It may bruise some egos, but the advice will be a little more in touch with reality.

MBAs

A lot of fuss was made in the early 1960s about the inadequacy of British management and a convenient scapegoat was found in the education system: not only in being the putative seed of the class division (also deemed a Bad Thing) but also to blame for the absence of sufficient specialist training. America was at the time the fashionable model and it had graduate business schools, so in Britain too management schools

proliferated. Thirty years and thousands of graduates later little has changed – the decline has continued inexorably and there is still a call for more and better training.[3]

We should not be surprised. The warnings and the attempted cures have been recurring with comforting regularity for about a hundred and fifty years. All that has changed has been the model chosen to emulate. Whoever was doing best at the time obviously had the right answers and should be copied wholesale with all practices and methods replicated in Britain.[4] Germany, France, the United States and Japan have all been models at some time. The notion that education, the class system and a uniquely British antipathy to practical things and trade also has a long ancestry.

The point about the MBA, like all training, is that it has to have a purpose and a measurable result.[5] With MBAs nobody has yet separated achievement between the two major factors: did someone do well from being a bright executive whose ambition saw a degree as a way of increasing expertise and opportunity, or because the education provided the disciplines needed by employers? For instance, it has been said Japan's most successful top industrialists lack business education, and management schools are in any case a waste of time.[6]

Larger companies which can afford to spare executive time sometimes reckon to send managers on courses to keep them up to date. Shrewd managers will question whether they are being groomed for promotion or being removed from the premises because they are dispensable, and the old man will be happy if someone has been bundled onto the course.

Tactics for executives Having an MBA has two useful functions: at recruitment it tells the prospective employer you are keen, and bright enough to get through the selection process; throughout the subsequent twenty years it allows you to pull intellectual rank.

If you do not have an MBA be sure to be sent on a course early in your career at a high-prestige business school (such as Fontainebleau, Harvard and the like). This will enable you to put down opponents in arguments with well-chosen quotations or attributions (which can be wholly bogus).

Do you want to go to hell with me, pig?

Physical training

In recent years there has also grown up a peculiar form of sadism which assumes that executives who survive a fortnight climbing Scottish mountains through blizzards dressed in a tee-shirt and shorts and living off a handful of hard-tack, will become miraculously better at purchasing stationery.

No sane person volunteers for such gratuitous torture and anyone nominated should develop serious lumbar problems immediately (very difficult to disprove) as a way of getting out of it. Indeed organisations managed by overgrown boy scouts who suggest pranks like that are probably best avoided.

Tactics for executives Avoid stress exercises whether physical or mental, especially where the purported aim is for managers to get to know each other. The last thing you want is for people in the organisation to get a glimpse of the real you.

The only sensible reason for going on such a course is to humiliate a boss or competitor; otherwise you can show your penetrating management analysis ability by subverting the whole insane process. The humiliation sustained by the opposition through your beating them or making them look absurd will probably entail cheating, but since nobody expects that in such games there is a good chance of it not being detected.

Another version is to encourage staff to play soldiers and leap through the bracken of Surrey shooting balls of paint at each other. Precisely what this encouragement of childish fantasies is supposed to achieve is not clear. Perhaps the powers-that-be feel that if there is another war the invaders will be repelled by serried ranks of production managers armed to the teeth with Dulux.

Management training

Francis Bacon pointed out nearly four hundred years ago (and it was probably a hoary old chestnut even by then) that 'it is esteemed a kind of dishonour unto learning to descend to enquiry or meditation upon matters mechanical'.

It may matter that getting your hands dirty in management is reckoned inferior to flamboyant parasitism in a service institution like accountancy, stockbroking or banking, but educating for management has always seemed dubious. Like being a footballer or violinist you either have the talent or you do not, and if you have, improvement comes from doing it rather than sitting and reading about it.

This may be why in the financial sector like the City of London (one of the rare sectors of British corporate activity that continuously generates a

substantial balance of payments surplus) there is practically no formal training. The nearest businesses seem to manage is what is traditionally known as `sitting next to Nelly'.

Admittedly the approach has had its critics. The stock exchange after a period of turbulence and public criticism decided to tighten the qualifications for being a stockbroker. And the recurrent bouts of scarcely credible incompetence by Lloyd's underwriters has been generally attributed to an unfortunate combination of innate stupidity and total absence of training in the assessment of risks. It may, however, be unfair to limit the blame to absence of adequate training: there was also a lamentable isolation from the realities of commerce outside Lime Street, but some training and examinations was reckoned to be part of the answer.

Lawyers and accountants already have to take stiff tests and bankers have an institute which sets papers. On the other hand if there is a statistically valid link between any form of education, training or type of instruction and financial success, nobody has yet spotted it.

Training further down the corporate hierarchy has had different problems. Just as everybody wants the government to spend less generally but more in every particular area, so training is approved of as a general principle but every company is reluctant to spend its own money on it.

Succession

What happens if the managing director gets knocked down by a bus? Few companies know; few managing directors care. It is astonishing to see powerful, driving, obsessed entrepreneurs flogging themselves to a standstill for twenty hours a day over forty years building up an enterprise,

yet giving not a moment's thought to keeping the thing going when the heart attack arrives. You would have thought they would want a more permanent memorial.

Perhaps they want to demonstrate to posterity their own indispensable genius – that without them even the most successful organisation reverts to chaos. Everybody knows this is in fact cobblers. As Clemenceau pointed out the cemeteries are full of indispensable people. Yet it is true that unless somebody plans ahead, large industrial groups run single-handedly by a forceful and charismatic autocrat stumble badly when he is removed. Despite that few such leaders make much provision for continuity except for half-hearted gestures at nepotism.

There are plenty of examples around us – libel laws prevent their being named – with the share price showing worry about the age of the top man if there is nobody evident to pick up the reins when he keels over.

Perhaps it is not just the implacable drive that built up the business that keeps the reins so convulsively clutched by its creator. Create an obvious successor and you create an assassin. There are plenty of incentives for ambitious young managers to plot the removal of ageing top people (see **Promotion**, page 45) without actually providing them with the means and the leader.

The same thing applies right through an organisation. Finance director, sales manager, foreman – all should in theory and for the good of the company start training their replacements. In practice it is tempting to succumb to inaction when faced with the dilemma of either *aprés moi le déluge*, or *et tu Brute*.

Since nurturing and preparing one's deputy requires the greater amount

of moral rectitude, dedication and energy, it is hardly surprising if self-interest allied to the line of least effort wins hands down. The result is that few senior people prepare the organisation for their eventual departure. The result is predictable confusion when they do go, whether on promotion or retirement. At best it occasionally happens that there is a mad scramble when a retirement approaches to make up for the previous ten years of inaction.

Organisations hate a vacuum and every time there is this sort of gap an unseemly jockeying develops which often produces visible strains that result in one of the promising contenders, and hence by definition a talented and useful manager, leaving in a huff at being passed over.

It is for all these reasons that every major organisation needs a tough and devious planner who is in charge of management succession.

Tactics for executives There are four main ways to get promoted: dead men's shoes, assassination, leapfrogging, or marrying the boss's daughter. (Some of these are discussed in **Promotion**, page 45.) Being trained and prepared to replace an existing manager demands planning.

One of the ways to show everybody you are being groomed and trained for swift advancement is by being sent to the troubled outposts of the corporate empire in your earliest days. When still raw and trying to make your name it is good to learn about company structure and to meet people farthest from head office. It is only later when you are capitalising on your widely publicised unique knowledge of the group that you need to be near the centre of power.

Communications

Are you talking to me?

Communications has become such a buzz-word that its meaning has been all but replaced by just a buzz, which is itself a rather nice illustration of what is wrong, a neat piece of recursive definition. People hear the word but fail to listen to what it means. The consequences are predictable – they get an eccentric and unfortunate view of what communication means.

Managers barking 'Get on with your work' think they are communicating. And so they are, but nothing very useful.

Communication notoriously needs not only a transmitter and a message but a receiver. Memories of domestic tiffs should remind us all how often there is a failure somewhere in the process, and somebody shouts or murmurs 'That is not what I meant at all. That is not it, at all'.

Obviously one of the problems may be that we are often woolly, vague and inarticulate. Or simply that the message is confusing or opaque because it has not been thought through. Just as good writing comes from good thinking, so clear communication of any sort comes from clear thought.

I How to make sure you are understood

Manner
A message can be confused by the method of trying to get it across. For instance, body language has been notoriously able to send a signal completely contradicting the verbal one. Even the cleverest liars find it hard to control their whole bodies and faces. As George Borrow warned 'Trust

not a man's words if you please or you may come to very erroneous conclusions; but all the time place implicit confidence in a man's countenance in which there is no deceit and of necessity there can be none.'

Tactics for executives In every encounter with other people watch for the subtle and unconscious signals which denote dislike, defensiveness or deceit. That means studying not just the details of the posture and gesture but also the faces and the positions of hands and legs of the people you encounter.

The double aim is to extract the unintended messages from others and to send out only those signals that you yourself intend to be received (whether they are accurate or not).[1]

Leaders and people of power have subtle but readily recognisable physical characteristics that most people absorb only subliminally.

Tone of voice, for instance. Confidence which comes from control and hence from power tends to make people relaxed so bodies and behaviour demonstrate this. Tension tends to constrict the throat and to raise the pitch of the voice. Recent research suggests that women's voices – at least when being publicly interviewed and recorded – have fallen quite noticeably in the past fifty years and this has been attributed to the greater confidence women now have in the public arena and in positions of power.

The obvious answer is to lower the pitch of your voice consciously to convey the air of relaxation and by implication confidence and power. This is a lesson taught to political figures by their image makers. If you doubt it listen to Lady Thatcher when she was just a member of parliament and when she became prime minister.

Such voice signals are obviously most important on the telephone. Pitch of voice, vocabulary, ease and friendliness of manner, and the degree of courtesy all send messages quite separate from the actual words.

People in authority do not need to talk fast. Obviously sharp and fast-moving minds produce rapid words but not a gabble. They can talk at their own speed because they expect to be listened to with interest and respect, and not be interrupted.

Posture is another guide. Confident success is signalled by walking tall with head carried high. Even to an untutored eye this conveys the air of someone who has accomplished much and is at ease. Nothing looks more defeated than a bowed head and slouch with dragging feet. Other things to avoid are signs of being on the defensive like crossed arms. Confident people also make more frequent and longer eye contact and have a lower blink rate.[2]

People are worth watching for other subtle signals. For instance, the pupils dilate when we see somebody (or something) we like and contract at a disliked object – hence the 'pinpoints of hate' that is the cliché for villains' eyes in cheap fiction. In a test of American college boys pictures of the same girls' faces were shown to two groups but some eyes had been retouched to produce small pupils and in others very dilated ones. In a very high proportion of cases the boys picked out the girls with large pupils as being sexier without realising the reason. That was why women used to put atropine drops in their eyes – it dilates pupils – which is in turn the reason it is called belladonna.

Other signals include body attitudes and direction, facial look, positions of hands and arms, placing of legs, and general posture. There are also gestures and the touching of the nose or ears, etc.

I'm a sucker for good conversation

Matter

Sometimes however not even the most piercing clarity of intellect combined with precise and carefully articulated message reaches its target. Try as you might you cannot get through.

Psychology has pinpointed one of the causes of the failure: literally a closed mind. If one holds beliefs and assumptions strongly enough, evidence that would contradict them sets up a tension that ensures the information is not perceived – not rejected, just not noticed at all.

It is called cognitive dissonance and the classic study on this was in the southern United States during segregation when a Japanese couple (officially designated coloured) in a huge chauffeur-driven limousine and with expensive leather luggage stayed the night at a hotel. During the subsequent interviews the hotel manager fervently and sincerely denied he had ever had coloured people to stay. The evidence clashed so strongly with his images that he could not reconcile them and his mind eased the strain by rejecting the data.

Tactics for executives You must therefore expect a level of incomprehension and misunderstanding and take precautions against it. One way is to surprise people into hearing what you are really saying, and the other is to finish by asking what people think they actually heard.

Having established by your manner and other ploys that you are a person to be considered and listened to, you must still make sure they really do hear what you are saying.

The unexpected frequently jolts people into a more receptive frame of mind. Open with a vivid phrase, a startling metaphor, an implausible

74

analogy or even a vulgar joke, and people are taken off guard. Look at how some novelists grab you from the first sentence:

> Despite my protests, Marietta revealed her breasts.
>
> (Gore Vidal, *Two Sisters*)

> It was a bright cold day in April and the clocks were striking thirteen.
>
> (George Orwell, *1984*)

> I was never so amazed in my life as when Sniffer drew his concealed weapon from its case and struck me down, stone dead.
>
> (Robertson Davies, *Murther and Walking Spirits*)

In every case the statement grabs you by the lapels and drags you in, making you more receptive for what is to come. It is a useful technique to learn – but not to use every time.

When the communication is actually a disagreement and you want to win an argument there are some very old ploys. One approach goes all the way back to Socrates and like him you can be unfair, arrogant, devious and plain dishonest in the way you use the tactic. Instead of asserting your own view over someone with whom you disagree you lead the other person to state their position and by carefully worded questions gradually force them to a paradox, contradiction or untenable consequence.

Successful Socratic dialogue requires forensic skill: the questions must be brief to the point of terseness and they must lead ineluctably but invisibly to your desired point of demonstrating how unacceptable the position is.

The converse of this approach is used when you are merely trying to

ensure you are getting through to a subordinate but it can also be an unsettling device when used to check whether your opponent in an argument has actually heard your case or refutation of his argument. This entails elucidating your own view and then checking whether the message has been precisely received. This is not by a peremptory demand: 'What have I just said?'. That is likely to produce a rude sound in response. You can for instance ask what a person dislikes about your view.

Managing subordinates

Winning the business battle requires the marshalling of subordinates into useful effort. That requires not just effective control but clear communications. Which method you use will depend on personal and corporate style; do you need to fit in or stand out?

Management by aggression and fear is certainly possible, and in some cases the best way. The army for instance has used it pretty effectively for centuries. Gradually, by experience, the army learned ideal-sized groupings: platoons of a dozen, squadrons of say three hundred, regiments of a thousand, and so on, with appropriate qualities of leadership – not brains as the army realised long ago that intellect is desirable only at the very top – for each level.

St Ignatius Loyola, founder of the Jesuit order, was closest to the military and was himself in turn copied by the Bolsheviks and then the Soviets. The pattern was also taken over by industry in the last century and worked well enough while employees were supine, obedient, poor and kept subservient by fear of unemployment. Prosperity has brought recalcitrance.

Times have so changed that even at times of high unemployment the

cajoling ingratiation of a sergeant major is unlikely to be popular or effective. For one thing employees can leave without being shot for desertion. For another, the military dictum that the men are not paid to think but to obey orders seldom produces the cosy cooperation desired in business.

Tactics for executives Managing by terror is likely to ricochet on managers – in the loss of good people, sabotage or vicious compliance. This last is an old problem caused by demanding unquestioning obedience and happens when the employee follows the rules with patient doggedness even though quite clearly able to see the machinery is stripping its threads, the computer spewing out acres of gibberish, and a prescribed procedure is manifestly creating a monumental foul-up.

In other words, running an organisation as if it were the army or the mediaeval Catholic church is grand so long as you can execute dissenters or worse still excommunicate them and so ensure damnation and torment for all eternity.

Early industrialisation assumed people hated work and responsibility, but liked security and had to be threatened and told what to do to ensure they worked towards the organisation's goals. An amazing number of companies operate as if they believed this still to be true.

With abject poverty and hence starvation receding so did such malleability. People jibbed at orders and preferred requests instead. As mechanical tasks were taken over by mechanisms employers needed cooperation and initiative.

'Scientific management' came in early this century and systematised

management principally by operating time and motion studies and installing piece rates.[3] Generally discredited by subsequent generations of management thinkers it is surprising how many of the ideas still linger tacitly in industrial practice. This is the management equivalent of something Keynes noted in economics: 'Practical men who believe themselves to be quite exempt from any intellectual influences, are usually the slaves of some defunct theoretician'.[4]

There have been many fads and theories of management since, each becoming ever more libertarian and participative.[5] As a result the executive should not be able to use the Eichmann defence: 'I was only doing what I was told'. If you are given a policy which is palpably rubbish you have to speak up and at the very least register your misgivings and doubts – and your subordinates should be encouraged to do the same.[6]

Nevertheless, for all the romantic desire of some observers for participative, liberal, consensus organisations, orders have to be given. Or as Peter Drucker put it 'Authority is an essential dimension of work' quite independent of structure.[7]

II The aim of communication

Communication has to have a purpose. For instance in business it may be:

- to spell out the task and what the job is
- a flow of information needed to carry out the task
- to report progress or completion
- feedback from subordinates
- to apportion praise or blame

Nothing is impossible for the man who doesn't have to do it himself

Delegation

The quality of managers is most clearly shown by the way and the amount they delegate. Good managers push down important decisions to good underlings; bad ones frazzle through muddle to cardiac arrest.

It takes confidence to delegate: self-confidence that it is neither an abdication of responsibility nor the creation of a claimant for one's job, and confidence that the people further down the structure are the right ones to do the job.

Managers who pride themselves on working eighty-hour weeks are frightened or inefficient. It is a constant delusion of the arrogant that nobody can cope as well as they and a fear of the insecure that they probably can.

One of the best ways of motivating people is to make work interesting and that means sharing responsibility. It also means encouraging people to delegate further down the line.

Tactics for executives The more work you delegate the less you will have to do yourself. In addition, you will have more time free for important activities like office politics.

But intelligent delegation goes beyond that: it motivates your staff to work harder. One of the ways is to spread the interesting work about a bit. It is poor teachers who always question the same pupils – the ones with their hands first in the air. So do not delegate only to the obvious stars, the ones eagerly clamouring for challenges. Some equally capable people may be shy, self-effacing or consider it vulgar to be too pushy.

Women in particular are prone to be passed over in this way because they tend to be less assertive and are reluctant to face rejection. Like other

more reserved executives they deserve to be given the chance to show their abilities. The organisation will benefit.

Information flow

Communication is rather more effective when two way, and that makes employees happier. People like being listened to[8] and they like being told what is going on.

A lovely example of this was in a teaching session for town clerks by a management consultancy. Despite their name town clerks are actually highly qualified, intelligent and powerful people. In this case they were split into three groups. The 'directors' were put into a carpeted room with plush chairs and luxuries; the 'managers' were put in a comfortable office; the 'workers' were put in a bare room with hard chairs and trestle tables.

The task was a relatively routine one involving complex ordering procedures but needed a constant stream of information from the managers who in turn got their instructions from the board. As an experiment the consultants severed the link between the workers and the rest, keeping them ignorant of how the work was developing and what part they were to play. Nor were they told how their next task was to be carried out. Within a very short time these men shed their sophisticated veneer and became such bolshy workers in their frustration that they ejected the consultancy observers, called a strike and marched out.

When the three groups were called together next morning for the briefing session, the consultant merely smiled and said 'I assume I do not need to explain to any of you the need for continuous communication'.

In the absence of two-way communication organisations ramble into

confusion and misunderstanding. Even when they all have similar aims confusion and conflict rule. Management guru Chris Argyris examined two hundred and sixty-five meetings at six companies and found executive behaviour created distrust and inflexibility even when their colleagues believed innovation was crucial.

They `unknowingly behaved in such a way as not to encourage risk-taking' partly to avoid conflict.[9] In the absence of openness and feedback from others in the organisation including subordinates, managers tend to become defensive and protect themselves from change.[10]

Feedback

An even more important reason for listening is that employees may have something useful to say. When Dunlop finally accepted it was incapable of running a tyre company and sold Fort Dunlop to Sumitomo the first thing the new Japanese management did was to ask the workforce for ideas. One junior worker had noticed years before that only every other fluorescent light was actually needed but nobody had been interested. His idea saved the new management £100,000 and helped to put the company in profit in thirty months.

One way management can really listen is by not waiting for workers to come to them but going where the employees are. An employee of a British television manufacturing plant taken over by the Japanese commented the new line managers occasionally worked a full shift on the production line. So while it had been easy to pull the wool over the British executives' eyes – they had hardly ever set foot on the shop floor – the new owners were wise to everything going on and knew precisely how long each operation took and how the manufacturing ran.

Tactics for executives Listen to employees even if you do nothing about their complaints and suggestions. They will often feel better simply for having got worries off their chests and it is better to vent these in talk than in some activity that could undermine your position.

Occasionally they may even come up with a good idea. You can then pat them on the head and take the credit.

Progress report
One of the purposes of communication is to tell people how they are getting on. People want to know what the boss thinks of them. Good or ill, they want acknowledgement of their existence.

Most people are uncertain of themselves and worry about their impact on other people. Indeed they seem to doubt their own existence. That is why people value something as trivial as a greeting and a thank you, and are profoundly upset and distressed (quite disproportionately from a logical standpoint) at being ignored.

You forgot to say 'please'   **Tactics for executives** The best way to acknowledge the worth of people, apart from the normal daily courtesies, is to provide a continuous flow of encouragement, incentive and guidance. Subordinates will perform prodigies with that sort of stroking.

The fundamental rule is: praise in public, blame in private. No matter how crass the confusion, irrespective of how stupid a mistake or how dangerous an action has been perpetrated, it is inexcusable to humiliate an employee in public. Shouting abuse in front of others, even in uncontrollable anger, is demeaning for both parties. Worse than that, it is ill-mannered.

Now there is a word you never encounter in textbooks or other learned literature on the subject – manners. Few attributes are more important, or more likely to oil even the rustiest of social wheels, yet the scholars and experts ignore it. For harmony in the office and good relations with people above, below and on either side nothing beats it.

Even if you have the power to order someone to do something, a courteous request will be received with gratitude, and a thank you when it is completed will be very welcome. As behavioural research on animals has shown, rewards provide a more effective incentive to preferred behaviour than punishments.[11]

Another aspect of this may be called discretion. That in particular extends to such things as affairs in the office.

Meetings are indispensable when you don't want to do anything

Meetings
Meetings are probably the most inefficient means of exchanging information or reaching a decision, and the larger the committee the more unlikely it is to produce any useful action. Harold Wilson once said Royal Commissions take minutes and waste years. It applies to all such waffle-sessions.

Tactics for executives It is a great mistake to think that just because committees are a total waste of time as far as practical achievement is concerned they should be ignored and boycotted. On the contrary, properly manipulated they can be very valuable to an ambitious executive.

The thing to remember is that what happens at the meeting is of only

peripheral interest. The main way of making sure meetings go your way is by the work you do before and after them.

That means getting on with the secretary of the committee. Before the meeting help to draw up the agenda and set the time for convening. If you have a particularly controversial or difficult item you want to go through on the nod, it must be scheduled immediately after something that everyone has views about and which is likely to raise an argument. When you attend, one of the jobs is to ensure the row is stoked to maximum pitch, preferably just short of physical violence. That means all the emotion and enthusiasm will have been drained and everyone will be exhausted in advance of your pet topic which can be slipped through almost unobserved.

The alternative is to make it the final item. If all the other matter on the agenda takes a very long time – which you can ensure – by the time your one arrives everyone will be rumbling for their lunch or raring to go home (depending on whether you opt for a morning or afternoon meeting). This is a more hazardous course as the committee may run out of patience and decide to defer the other items to the next meeting.

After the meeting you have to fix the minutes. Few people are going to remember precisely what they said and surprisingly often they will have little idea what if anything was decided. So if you help the secretary write the minutes you can explain what your understanding was of the various decisions taken. The only important message on this is not to let the power go to your head – distort only the items of importance to minimise the chances of a retaliation.

Pay

If you pay peanuts you get monkeys

A grave infection of puritan envy masquerading as love of justice has been afflicting the national press. Any chairman or senior executive with high or fast-rising pay is automatically vilified. The public odium is heaped on even if the company has performed startlingly well and the pay rose as a result of a profit-related bonus.

In the real world of business, pay is set by the market. Greed does not prosper long. If the executive does not deliver, not just the pay but the job is forfeit. It may take a while but shareholders, especially of financial institutions, will not long tolerate conspicuous consumption at their expense.

I Executive salaries

Even allowing for the normal proportion of humbug from commentators, there is a lot of hypocrisy from the top men about it not being all salary. Actually it is never called pay or salary anyway – it may be a remuneration package, reward, compensation, and so on. Anyway, the executives plead the package had an element of pension contributions, share options, bonuses, etc. As if that made a scrap of difference.

The next piece of flannel is the disingenuous statement that top salaries are set by the non-executive directors. Considering what a supine bunch of beached jellyfish non-execs have shown themselves to be over recent years, this is hardly a convincing argument. Indeed, so fatuously ineffective have remuneration committees been it is intriguing to check where

members come from. And sure enough, they are executives on other boards where their own salaries are no doubt set by non-execs who are themselves executives elsewhere. Backs must be raw from all that scratching.

As top salaries soar out of the stratosphere they provoke resentment in the rest of the organisation. Executives may need to defend their pay with two arguments: the best is never cheap and the cheap is always too expensive; and people can make a lot of money only if they provide goods and services of the sort and quality that a public is prepared to pay for.

Fees paid to a merchant bank may seem a bit steep at a couple of million quid to handle an acquisition, yet companies are prepared to pay although they could probably find somebody prepared to act for a quarter of the money. The customer reckons to be getting expertise and safety.

When salaries and fees streak away in a blue blur, however, there is a truculent vulgarity about it that suggests the individual is more concerned about the feathers of a personal nest than about the corporate tree.

When the pay starts soaring to £250,000 or £500,000 a year hackles begin to rise and mutterings start about sheer damn avarice, and whether anybody is really worth that much.

In the majority of cases it is less the absolute levels which generate the greatest bitterness, though these do invite unwelcome scrutiny at Himalayan altitudes, it is the comparisons that grate.

The part of the protest that is not merely hypocrisy stems from some notion of equity. This in turn derives from vague feelings of what is a reasonable purchasing power[1] and some ideas about the division of the corporate cake.

Purchasing power is the point. Parkinson's second law – `expenditure rises to meet income'[2] – is the delightful optimism of the ordered and

86

Those who tell you it's tough at the top have never been at the bottom

affluent. For some of us there is always some month left over at the end of the salary. Becket's variant might be: spending swamps income.

To put it another way, every rise in pay merely catches up on part of the accumulated debt – but only as a short-term measure. By the time the rise arrives it has long been spent.

Pay is an emotive issue for other reasons as well. It indicates how highly a person's contribution is rated and so goes to the heart of acceptance and self-esteem. Money may not be an adequate measure of effectiveness, but there is no satisfactory alternative. So people watch the relativities with penetrating care to see how well regarded they currently are.

Performance-related pay is a powerful inducement to effort even outside production where it has been most widely used. It must however be related to achievement and therefore sits uneasily on jobs and areas where the individual's effect on success is remote.

Even where it does apply it needs a few simple rules:

- the system must be acknowledged fair, both on thresholds/ratios and amount
- the accounting system must be transparent, with pre-agreed computations, including apportionment of overheads
- the base salary needs to be reasonable if not generous
- no ceiling is to be set on bonuses even if they get embarrassingly high
- permanent proportion of pre-tax profit is set aside for bonuses
- even when the company as a whole is doing badly some people and some sections may be performing well enough to deserve a bonus
- where contribution to profit is not applicable supervisors give merit rises for which they account to their superiors

- executive perks should be avoided – pay people cash

II Sales representatives

Traditionally sales representatives are paid on commission. To provide a real incentive that should be on a sliding scale – say three per cent on the first £50,000, five per cent on the next £50,000, and so on.

On occasions, in a year that combines good luck with lots of hard work, a salesman may get more than directors. Quite right too. Recently the man who invented and runs Direct Line insurance for Royal Bank of Scotland was paid about ten times as much as the chief executive.

Be careful to set targets at the right level in the first place, because it gets hard to adjust later. A classic recent example of that was of a communications company which found so many salesmen were reaching its targets it had to pay substantial sums in commissions so it decided to raise the thresholds. Three of its top four salesmen promptly left.

Such high pay for salesmen may also prove a salutary disincentive to promoting them (see **Promotion**, page 45). Successful barristers consent to being made judges – which can mean a pay drop of up to eighty per cent – once they have amassed a reasonable pile, feel their business beginning to drift away, or would like a pension please. There is a great danger of that with the good field workers as well.

Tactics for directors   Since so much attention is being focused on board salaries good public relations practice suggests it would be wise to evade such unwelcome attention. Clearly, the choice of taking lower pay is out of

the question so some moves need to be worked out in advance.

One is to have a contract of under a year because that does not require the details to be disclosed at the annual general meeting. This however can have unpleasant consequences at times of strife.

Casual, non-contractual consultancy work for one or more of the subsidiaries may help to make up the pay packet.

Setting levels

Setting the actual level of pay is not very difficult. Two criteria guide the level: the prevailing market rate, and a decision on whether one is aiming for short-term results (set pay at minimum needed to recruit and give no rises if possible) or long-term performance (pay enough for staff to feel you are generous or at least fair).

Finding the market rate is a matter of minimal research. If there are not enough advertisements or statistics to indicate what others are prepared to pay, and if neither statistics nor competitors are forthcoming, you can try the auction approach of offering absurdly low pay and raising it until a satisfactory applicant appears.

Some occupations have such an aura of charm and prestige or offer such attractive fringe benefits that people flock to them for the glamour rather than the pay. As a result, companies in advertising, journalism and publishing would be stupid to pay more than a pittance. On the other hand if you want the best it comes highly priced but not necessarily expensive and even in those sought-after areas the stars who are scarce and fetch in the customers – brilliant copywriters, popular columnists, successful editors – get paid pretty well. In some cases very well indeed, thank you.

Make my day

Tactics for executives Getting a pay rise presents an exciting challenge. Traditionally the two routes are either for the boss to decide you are doing an exceptionally good job and decide an increase has been well merited, or for you to go in and suggest you are worth more.

Clearly the former is preferable because the boss imagines it to be a spontaneous idea and a generous gesture. Such intellect and magnanimity provide a self-righteous glow of altruism which will increase the boss's kindly thoughts towards you. It is indeed more blessed to give than to receive for we always feel well towards people we can patronise. By contrast few people can forgive a favour done them. The tactic must therefore be to drive thoughts ineluctably in that direction without exciting a suspicion that such a notion is anything but wholly self-induced. This can be by:

- just keeping your head down and doing the job exceedingly well
- getting somebody to suggest to the boss you are worth more
- making the boss feel you might leave for a better offer
- accepting it as an alternative to deserved promotion

Hard work
Just doing the job with unostentatious diligence and competence is a futile policy unless the boss is a selfless, percipient, humane and sensitive believer in justice. Such saints are relatively rare in business.

Even if you are by nature the dedicated conscientious type with a fascination for the job in hand, it is at the very least sensible to ensure that somebody notices.

This route has always been a failure in career terms. It merely gets you taken for granted and instead of more money you get more work.

Let's hustle

Internal PR

If current office conditions make overt approaches imprudent, or if a well-bred aversion to praising yourself makes the technique impossible, you have to find a surrogate. At the simplest level this means making friends with somebody in the organisation who is in a position to suggest to your boss that you are worth quite a lot more – and is prepared to do it. On the other hand the chances of grabbing the friendship of someone with the boss's ear and the desire and detached benevolence to praise you are pretty remote.

The effect can be achieved by other means. Someone thanks you for a favour or for help and says how wonderful you are. Do not respond with a deprecating gesture; say 'Don't tell me, tell my boss'. Most people will merely smile, but sooner or later some of them will pass on the praise. This applies with even greater force to encounters further up the management tree.

Such an approach works just as well for promotion and you can help both by getting close to your boss's boss. In **Promotion** this was suggested as the way up either by supplanting or leapfrogging one's immediate superior. As a preliminary or (at the worst) an alternative to promotion such links can help prompt improvements in pay if not in position.

Possible departure

How you demonstrate your obvious desirability depends on the audience. Some top executives bridle at what they see as blatant blackmail when an employee marches in to announce a better offer elsewhere. Some respond to nothing more subtle. In businesses where frequency of movement is

Lunch is for wimps

normal, for example advertising and the media, open demands or ultimata are common currency.

For executives and occupations lacking such familiarity with real life you have to activate rumour. Before starting either course though do make sure to have an exit route if the campaign goes disastrously awry. This is the secret of all business planning and all good generalship. Contingency planning is vital. 'The wise general, even the most courageous, will keep in mind the possibility of failure or defeat and will plan for them' warned the last Roman emperor Mauricius Flavius Tiberius.[3]

Since we are here talking about the boss getting the idea wholly spontaneously that you are invaluable or at least worth more, it might be nice to make him feel you are wanted. The usual system is to give the impression you are desperately trying to cover up the fact that you are being pursued by a headhunter.

If you are going to arrange for telephone calls seemingly to come from people offering you jobs be very careful in your choice of public evasions.

The same applies to sneaking out for 'covert' lunches. In some circumstances getting the reputation for bedding interesting people can enhance your status but it is a dangerous game to play.

Consolation prize
Never give up the prospects for promotion, but it is only realistic to acknowledge when the immediate chances are remote. If none of the internal jobs you want are likely to be vacant for at least a couple of years it is even more important for the top echelons in the company to realise your claims to advancement.

All life is a game of power. The object of the game is simple enough: to know what you want and get it

You certainly need to keep yourself in the public eye when promotion is finally available and in the meantime get a rise while making the top people feel they still owe you one.

III Fringe benefits

The range of fringe benefits, perks and corporate back handers is enormous and seldom justifiable on any rational basis. Despite government discouragement, including a growing proportion of tax on such benefits in kind, and in spite of the high cost and a fair amount of resentment from workers deprived of such goodies, the complex system in Britain has grown to be the largest among the industrialised countries.

One reason is that companies think it is cheaper than handing over money, and they feel it has greater motivating power. As a result, some of the popular perks are (in no particular order):

- company car
- private medical insurance
- extra annual holidays
- non-contributory pension scheme
- interest-free season ticket loans
- loans and mortgages at subsidised interest rates
- free membership of clubs and/or professional bodies
- annual shindigs (sorry, conferences) at luxurious resorts
- tickets to Wimbledon, Covent Garden, the Varsity rugby match, the Cup Final, Royal Ascot, etc.

- free life assurance
- subsidised meals (ranging from Luncheon Vouchers to canteen)
- share option scheme
- free or cut-price membership of a health club
- subsidised holidays

This is the sort of thing that tends to run away with the company and removes itself from all control by top management. At that stage it gets to be expensive, nobody can tell whether the package is still tax-efficient, and since everybody has grown to expect it any motivational factor has long since evaporated.

One item in that list however is probably worth retaining when other perks fail to justify their survival: giving managers and other employees a chance to buy the shares. Not only do they feel more part of the organisation, but their attitudes are transformed. If you find one employee rebuking another for leaving the lights on or wasting time or stationery, you may be sure he owns a chunk of the equity.

Most such perks have traditionally been for management. For a long time most workers have preferred cash in hand to more remote fringe benefits such as pensions enhancements, but privatisations and government encouragement are now spreading the practice of share ownership.

Secretaries

One perk seldom recognised as such is the executive secretary. The manager gets a factotum who operates as nanny and housekeeper, clerk and waitress, sister and guard dog without real economic justification for such cosseting. Secretaries are an expensive, inefficient and badly used

executive fringe benefit and should be one of the earliest to be reformed.

Secretaries command salaries depending on the market and quite independent of their ability to type or take shorthand (few of them can). One way to save money on this asset is to deprive top managers of their own secretaries. No secretary is fully occupied unless she is doing a large chunk of her boss's work (which to be fair many do) so it is far more efficient to use scarce resources by allocating say six secretaries to ten managers.

That has the added advantage of having somebody to answer phones throughout the day, even at lunchtime, allows for holidays, and the secretaries, not being isolated in an avoided and remote private office, provide a full day's work, and enjoy the variety and company.

Titles

Another method of reward (cheaper than cash or perks) is by titles. They have three useful functions:

- as an alternative to a pay rise
- to make employees feel good
- to fool customers

The public sector has long realised the benefits of scattering KCMGs to functionaries. Whitehall has managed to go on attracting good brains without bothering to compete on pay by offering interesting work, security, a good pension and reasonable certainty of a gong. Back-bench MPs are kept in line not only by their own stupidity, but by the assurance of a knighthood or, if they are spectacularly useless, a life peerage.

Public figures are prepared to make good the deficiencies of state safety

Making money is fun, but it's pointless if you don't use the power it brings

nets with generous altruism thanks to the prospect of similar baubles. It is quite amazing just how much they are prepared to donate to a wide variety of charities in the certain knowledge that unless they are actually caught with their fingers in the till they will certainly be given some honour.

There is no reason why companies cannot emulate this and there are signs of it happening. We have now not only managing directors, but also chief executives and also chief operating officers; not just chairmen but vice-chairmen, deputy chairmen, and presidents. People seem to have an insatiable appetite for titles and gewgaws no matter how spurious. So, since it costs nothing, why stint on them?

Some merchant banks are knee-deep in managing directors not because their senior staff need to be fooled by titles (they get money), but because it impresses customers. Everybody always wants the attention of a top executive and an inflation in labels means a mere director is often no longer impressive enough.

Tactics for executives The way to get a good starting salary is through the techniques of the souk. Argue for the maximum, pretend not to be interested in less, and when you have reached a genuine impasse switch the haggling to other and additional rewards. These include payments by results, share options, promotion, etc. Come armed with statistics, no matter how spurious. Have information about competitors, no matter how distorted.

Working Environment

If you can count your money you don't have a million dollars

I Premises

All management manuals say you must provide good premises if you want good work. Huge textbooks have been written on minute details of ergonomics and the working environment ranging from the ideal chair height to the precise position of a computer keyboard on the desk. Expensive studies over decades have examined the effects of colours in decorative schemes. They have looked at the levels of light, the arrangement of furniture and background sounds. Experiments have been carried out with ionising the working atmosphere and the introduction of subtle smells.

Whatever other conclusions have been reached by highly paid designers and social scientists, they all seem to agree that a good (ie. expensive) environment is needed to encourage good work. Apart from a cynical suspicion that it would be hard to justify their fees with any other conclusion (which would also deprive them of further work), it sounds sensible and humane, even obvious. But in fact it is rubbish – a waste of money.

Tactics for directors So long as the spirit is right and the management is seen to care, people will work in Dickensian squalor and revel in it. It is worth remembering that it was only after they moved out of their sheds and garages and into elegant corporate headquarters that computer companies like Acorn and Apple ran into trouble.

Look at publishing: intelligent, charming and highly educated people

C'est magnifique, mais ce n'est pas la guerre

work dedicatedly for a pittance despite being jammed into insanitary hovels. Visit a successful research establishment: debris-ridden sheds at inaccessible sites contain people prepared to work through their holidays.

Bill Mackey, who as head of insolvency at accountancy firm Ernst & Young was for decades Britain's leading corporate undertaker, distilled a lifetime's experience into seventeen widely acclaimed symptoms of impending disaster. There were the signs of companies where arrogance, self-importance and dignity had taken over from maximising profit. Three of Bill Mackey's indicators of imminent failure relate to premises: fountain in the reception area; flagpole outside the factory; and new offices opened by prime minister.[1]

C. Northcote Parkinson in his famous book *Parkinson's Law*[2] spelled it out even more forcefully. When you come across a company with perfect, beautiful offices full of art, highly designed fittings and ankle-deep carpets you have not discovered prosperous efficiency: 'It is now known that a perfection of planned layout is achieved only by institutions on the point of collapse.' They are of course both absolutely right.

The classic experiment demonstrating the truth of these insights was at the Hawthorne Plant of Western Electric[3] in Chicago. A team from Harvard tried to discover the optimum rest periods and lighting level for manufacturing. They raised the light level and, as expected, output rose. They increased it again and production rose as well. They intensified the light still further, and sure enough production improved yet again. By this time the light was blindingly bright so the clever Harvard chaps lowered the level. To their consternation the workers produced still more. Moreover the control group, whose lighting had remained unchanged, also improved productivity.

At this point they decided to investigate a little more carefully. Puzzled, they found employees were so delighted management cared enough to consult them, observe how they felt, and took so much time and trouble to improve working conditions that output rose with morale.

The lesson of all that is not that one should impose unnecessary squalor on employees, but that it is more important to be seen to care about their welfare than to provide plush comfort or ostentatious luxury. But as with all generalisations, there are exceptions.

Financial centres are different. Whether trading in shares, cocoa futures, currencies, gold or treaty retrocession on excess of loss for cargo hulls, all you need is contact with customers (telephone), some idea of the shifting market (information onto screens), and a way of working out your margins (calculator). But instead of the phone booths which could accommodate all that, sited in cheap suburban property, such people get palatial new purpose-built temples in the most expensive acreage in the world.

That is all just part of the paradox of pay: the nastier, dirtier and more dangerous a job the less it is paid, while clean, stimulating work of power, influence and fun provides absurd salaries. Compare the pay of a dustman with a bond dealer, a deep-sea fisherman with a merchant banker. So, dangerous and badly paid jobs are also done in harsh unpleasant surroundings while highly paid work that gives you a buzz is in accessible places and delightful surroundings.

The notional desk

In some types of job there ought to be no working environment at all. IBM for instance has taken on board the notion of the `virtual desk' dreamed up in

Being powerful is like being a lady: if you have to tell people you are, you ain't

management consultancy some twenty years ago. On the principle that consultants, like salesmen, ought hardly ever to be in the office, there is little point in wasting expensive space by reserving desks, computer terminals etc, for them. Instead there are, say, three spare desks among every couple of dozen of such people and if they do happen to be in the office they sit wherever there is an empty chair.

The legal burden

Work places are governed by a cat's cradle of legislation which is being supplemented almost daily by creative ideas from Brussels. Only recently, for instance, the European Community set very tight standards on the quality of computer screens and the levels of light and radiation they emit.[4]

While some safety aspects are laid down in minute and terrifying detail (the provision of fire exits and other precautions for example), employees are surprisingly enough presumed to be grown ups with some sense and the company is not expected to be nanny to 'an imbecile child'.[5] The regulations merely spell out how to avoid trouble and say as near nothing as makes any difference about what precisely are the right sort of business premises. What all this means in effect is that the place must be safe and reasonably comfortable; it must not be too hot or cold, damp or noisy.

Specifying what a good working environment comprises is almost impossible. On the other hand there are some easily specifiable things to avoid both in the way of premises and general company practice:

- muzak unless it is to cover the gibberings of the insane
- widely discrepant feeding arrangements for directors and workers
- reserved parking spaces – important people should get there first

Some companies have a nice line in packaged responses: you add a set of ingredients and everything will work out for the best. So they put potted plants into the open plan offices; they introduce a company house magazine; they paint some areas gaudy nursery colours; they organise jollies at sun-drenched resorts for top executives and dinners in town for the workers.

In fact even on their own many of these things are not only unnecessary, but counterproductive. House magazines, for instance, may reassure a few clerical workers, but generally make for an expensive way to invite contempt.

Tactics for executives Just as one's personal appearance provides clues to status and class, so the workplace is a good indication of an executive's position and power. The Civil Service has predictably refined this with elaborate precision. Clues include not only the colour of the carpet, but whether it stretches wall-to-wall, whether one's room contains a hat stand, and whether there are any extra chairs in the room and if so of what number and type. All these show visitors the precise rank of the occupant.

Other offices have different but well-known signals: the type of telephone, size of desk, sort of chair, presence of lamps and computers are all apportioned on the basis of status. Knowing these it is easy to disorient people by smuggling in unauthorised indicators of rank.

If you can do no more than make people uneasy about your precise position, it will have been worth while. Is that extra, unlabelled telephone really a direct line to the chairman/Bank of England/10 Downing Street/ Buckingham Palace (invent your own, but reasonably plausible, fantasy), or

merely a dummy? In any case always have an extra telephone line on your desk, preferably a cellphone in a charger, and have your own answering machine on your extension.

Executive toys like clicking stainless-steel ball bearings are definitely to be avoided – you have no time for that sort of frivolity. But the desk should always have on it a few files in vivid colours marked STRICTLY CONFIDENTIAL in large letters.

Furnishing the rest of the office is also important. Some furniture in itself carries subtle clues of status – high-backed chairs for instance and ones that swivel. In addition you must always ensure your own chair is several inches higher than any visitor's chair. Better still, have a low sofa for visitors to sit on.

There is a division of opinion on the best location for an office or desk. One view is that it is best to be near the seat of power where one can be continuously noticed by the top people and can even chat to them occasionally on a casual and unofficial basis. The theory is that people who are always apparent come to mind first when there are interesting jobs to be filled, or promotion in the offing. This policy dictates getting a space on the executive floor, even if it is only a broom cupboard. In open plan offices it means being at a desk where the boss can see you and where he has to pass by several times a day. There are ways of finding such a prime position legitimately, but they tend to be a hassle and can lead to elaborate arguments so bribery and subterfuge are better.

The other tactic is to go off into a totally forgotten corner, perhaps into another building altogether, but as far from supervision as possible. This is the solution if you intend to start your own little entrepreneurial activity

within the company, pursue your own set of policies, deal with your own products, and hire your own staff. In most large organisations you can get away with a lot of this sort of independence, but you have to knit up the results and make the project watertight if you are to win eventual credit for its achievements.

II Organisations

In addition to the physical environment, there is the psychological or organisational structure. This has been a fertile ground for management theorists for generations, indeed possibly for centuries.[6] All this has produced are diffuse and contradictory sets of conclusions, none of which has been shown to be right.[7]

Tactics for executives   The first thing to remember about organisation theory is that the corollary to nothing having been proved right is that nothing has been proved wrong. Some theories suit the circumstances of a particular market, a company or a set of individuals, but not absolutely and not for ever.

So, if you want to make your name as an innovative, wide-thinking, and energetic manager, put forward a plan for changing the organisation structure. Every company should be reorganised at about seven year intervals. It is not that centralisation is better than delegating authority to autonomous units at the periphery, or vice versa, but that people need to be jolted out of their dozy complacency from time to time.[8]

Staff Turnover

Through? I haven't even started

I Turnover

It is always the wrong people who leave. The useless, stupid and idle have neither the energy nor the persuasive ability to get another job; the bright, active and successful are being lured continuously by others. As a result, a sensible organisation keeps a careful check on staff turnover because one day it will be a sound way of predicting major problems looming up. It will also pinpoint the area of the probable problem.

Tactics for directors   Assuming there is a better than even chance of the business surviving, it would be sensible for management to start to look at three things:

- what is going wrong that so many useful people want to go?
- how much will it cost to recruit and train replacements for the dear departed?
- do they really need to be replaced precisely or is this an opportunity to shift the direction and emphasis?

What is wrong?

To find the cause of a departure the emigration interview should not be by the person's immediate boss – that may well be where the principal problem lies – but by someone at least one level further up the structure. Quite a lot can be gleaned from such a chat because the person leaving no

longer feels inhibited by fear of losing a pay rise or even the job. That can make them positively garrulous as they unpack years of frustrated observation and suggestions, are forthcoming in analyses of how things could be done better and reveal what might have persuaded them to stay.

They will also provide interesting evaluations not just of working practices but of people as well, both colleagues (no longer fearing reprisals) and superiors. They will know, and with careful inducement may say, who is lazy, mendacious, sex-obsessed and crooked.

As with all interviews, however, there is no reason to believe everything the person says. The chance of settling old scores without the danger of retaliation may be too strong. There is also the converse danger of nostalgia with all the preposterous transformation of misremembered misery into survival of shared hardships.

Finally, they may just be wrong. Not everybody is accurate in assessing character or even in interpreting facts. In any case, even if the information is accurate, not malicious and correctly interpreted, it must be used with some circumspection. The main question is, does it matter? The secondary one is, what can we do to offset the shortcomings? For instance, having an employee with an apparently insatiable sexual appetite is only a problem if it gets in the way of work. At least knowing the problem means a careful manager can keep temptation out the worker's way or ensure the passion is not indulged during working hours.

Despite such handicaps and the need for such allowances, even the briefest conversation can be surprisingly revealing. If supplemented by factual analysis of the departure, a picture should begin to emerge. Facts required include such details as department, immediate boss, time of year, pay level etc.

The cause can be as simple as inadequate pay, or it may be that one or more manager is impossible to work with. Corporate structure may be almost calculated to frustrate ambition in able people; corporate policy may be so fatuous no bright executive can long bear to see such a waste of resources. Or it may just be a time of thriving commercial activity with high labour turnover. No simple single factor is likely to be the cause but motivation (see **Discipline**, page 30) is almost certain to be part of it.

Cost of replacement
There is no point acquiring information except to some purpose. Having found out why people leave, one needs to decide whether that is regrettable. Even accepting the best people are most likely to go, if able young recruits are prepared to fill vacancies at pathetically low pay, the company may well take a rational decision that the danger is acceptable and benefits outweigh the shortcomings.

A rational decision requires facts and the direct costs of replacement are easy to find. Advertising vacancies, staff time for interviews and selection etc, are a doddle to cost. Indirect costs like the loss of business or the inferior quality of work from new recruits is harder to put a precise figure on. It is worth making the effort – the figures may be rough and inaccurate but they do at least provide a starting point for doing the calculations.

Once the figures are available, no matter how rough, those costs can readily be set against the price of an alternative strategy. Would it be worth paying the incumbent a higher salary (assuming that is the problem) to prevent their departure? Is it cheaper to change procedures or working practices (if that is demanded) than suffer a fifteen per cent wastage of staff?

The team effort is a lot of people doing what I say

There is also the converse. If there is a manager who gets so far up people's noses he puts their backs up, should he be moved sideways to somewhere he can do less harm, severely censured (which might make him leave in disgust) or even sacked? The alternatives can be costed and then compared with the performance of the manager you already have to see whether the exercise is worth it.

Replace or reorganise?
It is a cliché, and therefore possibly true, that a problem to a failure is an opportunity for a success. So coping with staff turnover provides an executive with a wonderful chance to change tack, improve methods or create new approaches.

For instance, a shrewd manager can use the departure of an obviously able subordinate to impress on the board that the section is both underpaid and so overworked not even the hardworking and clever can cope. This not only draws attention to the keenness and effort of the whole section, including oneself of course, but permits the increase of an empire.

Tactics for executives   Keep a shrewd eye on who is leaving and where they are going; such knowledge may present chances for promotion and useful sideways moves. At the very least it will show where vacancies are likely to occur, which in itself is useful. You can tip someone off about the job going and earn a favour in return. Alternatively you can import your own nominee and thereby build up a private guard beholden to you. Finally of course it provides hints about promotion for yourself.

On another level, if it starts looking like a major exodus, the alert manager

may start wondering why so many sleek rats are striking for the shore. When he discovers the reason he may want to join them.

An executive thinking of jumping ship needs to prepare to make sure he doesn't land in the middle of the ocean. Or indeed that he is not obliged to walk the plank before a safe landing place has been prepared.

Just putting out the word that one is open to attractive offers can quickly leak back to a boss who may then wonder if enthusiasm may be waning. The answer therefore is either to target the precise company and the precise person in it to approach, or to get a headhunter to do it. The advantage of doing it yourself is that you are in full control, the disadvantage is of putting oneself through a lot of useless and wearying effort merely to face repeated rejection. The advantage of a headhunter is subcontracting the hard labour to a professional, the disadvantage is that unless you are a highly desirable and visible star headhunters may go through the polite motions but they will not even take you onto their books.

Executive searchers also tend to assume the brilliant people they are looking for are so desirable they are unlikely to be looking for a job. It is the Groucho Marx type of problem: he would not belong to an organisation that would accept him as a member; headhunters do not want the sort of people who want to be found by them.

There are companies which purport to act the other way and find jobs for people – avoid them. For the most part they are expensive and useless. Some will charge inordinate amounts to help compile a CV and teach applicants how to sound plausible at an interview, but there are no reports of any being successful. Executives tempted by desperation into the den of this sort of charlatan should insist on paying by results.

If the exploration is merely to find an alternative offer as a way of screwing a better deal out of the present employer, even greater tact is needed (see **Pay**, page 85). For a kick-off just make sure the other job is at least acceptable in case the boss calls your bluff: 'I've had a rather handsome offer from Bloggins & Snooks to be their special projects manager.'

'Oh really. How splendid for you. I hope you'll be very happy there.'

II Redundancy

Sometimes the departures are not the employees' idea. Nor have they been for misconduct (see **Discipline** for that). During recent recessions managers have been heard to wander round the offices in a slightly dazed state, muttering 'Is there any truth in the rumour I've resigned?'

Redundo became a way of life. On the other hand this can be an expensive way of saving money for the company since any worker of more than two years' standing is entitled to compensation. Some have therefore gone to wonderfully subtle lengths to persuade people to resign.

To prevent employees from having their lives made a misery by the devious ploys of such businesses the law has invented the ingenious notion of constructive dismissal. This is the very opposite of dismissal in fact, since the employee is kept on the staff – just. For instance demotion,[1] accusing a worker of theft,[2] swearing at him,[3] or giving him a rotten office[4] counts as constructive dismissal. Putting a night-shift worker onto day-shifts[5] can have the same effect.

Once again there are opportunities here for the shrewd and unscrupulous.

109

Fasten your seat belts – it's going to be a bumpy ride

It takes strong nerves to work in an organisation that is so deeply troubled it is sacking people in such a desperate and comprehensive fashion, taking broad sabre slices from top to bottom of the corporate structure. To stay you need the confidence to know the company will survive; that you will keep your job in it; and that many of the managers senior to you will be lopped off.

Quite recently a relatively junior manager in a specialised corner of a major City institution suddenly found himself managing director as eight top people were landed with the blame for a series of losses.

Tactics for executives To stay on at a crumbling outfit in the expectation of being the one remaining candidate for senior responsibility untainted by the crass conduct of the board and so being the only one left for promotion, is a high-risk approach and requires careful preparation.

If you really have decided that there is benefit in hanging on (and that you are not following that course out of cowardice or apathy), work out well in advance how you are going to survive.

Experience also teaches that even if the strategy succeeds you are unlikely to be allowed to stay long. In such panics top people are changed more rapidly than socks.

Eventually a butcher or `company doctor' is usually brought in from outside to reconstruct the business from scratch and to sack anyone who was present at the time of the debacle. But having got there the departure will at least be accompanied by a golden handshake. (See **Discipline** on page 30 for how to extract the best terms.) Despite the generosity of such pay-offs some executives may dislike the public parting and possible association with failure.

110

An alternative is to leave before the fan gets clogged. A shrewd executive will see axes being whetted and look for another job. But do not be tempted to resign and go to a better, safer hole. Ease your way to the front of the queue to be made redundant (perhaps you could even volunteer for it) because that can produce a nice fat departure present and can be agreed amicably in private.

III Absenteeism

A professor of industrial relations at Columbia University in New York came to Britain in the early 1960s to study absenteeism among miners. It was a major problem and famously intractable.

On a Monday morning – always the peak for absences – he took a random list of those who had not turned up and went round to their homes. A typical encounter found the miner perfectly healthy with his feet up in front of the television. Why are you not at work, asked the professor. The miner would wave his hand at the picture window of the spacious council flat. `See, across there? I was born in one of those crumbling back-to-backs. Now I live here. Down there, that shiny new Ford? That's mine. Up there, just beyond the trees, is the nice new school where my kids are. In two months' time we are off to Spain for our holidays. Why should I flog myself to a standstill for a few measly quid I don't really need?'

Such sentiments shook the professor brought up on the Protestant work ethic. He decided to seek explanation in the context and travelled south to observe managers and white-collar workers.

In America, he explained, every executive is busting a gut to make vice-

president. He works every hour God sends, and ruptures every sinew to win promotion. In Britain, he discovered, the most common ambition among senior executives was to become a gentleman farmer.

Ruefully the professor admitted he knew which was best for the country, but which attitude was best for the individual was a more difficult problem.

The point of all this is to show absenteeism as often as not stems from a fundamentally English approach (the Scots and the Welsh seem to have a more serious attitude to work, though they too are being corrupted). To offset such understandable reluctance to procure an early grave by excessive effort demands sophisticated motivation or draconian disincentives.

Another point is that applying formulae from experts, most of whom learned their theories from overseas studies, is unlikely to change much.

Tactics for executives Never stay off work for just one day with the pretext of an illness. That confirms to everyone it was merely an unusually bad hangover. Two days is the minimum, but preferably make it three.

Other excuses should be imaginative, but not so spectacularly as to draw attention to the ingenuity. A wife going into labour is acceptable, but not more than twice a year. A close relative dying is plausible, but only once every four years. A water burst at home is credible, but only if there has not been a gas explosion, a burglary and a fire in the past ten months.

International Relations

What is important is not where you came from, but where you're going to

Few countries have a more colourful or extensive vocabulary of xenophobia than Britain. For centuries the language has proliferated with exuberant political incorrectness: frogs, wogs, dagoes, krauts, wops, yids, niggers, hun, chinks, nips; few peoples escape the contemptuous vitriol of traditional prejudice. Indeed, so profound is this distaste for anything even vaguely unusual that it flourishes even within the British Isles: sassenach, grockle, bogtrotter and so on.

Perhaps it is caused by the ingrained disdain for the opinions of foreigners but there is an irony in the failure of this name-calling to work in reverse. In the far east the British regularly refer to themselves as gwailo, the Chinese term of contempt for foreign devils; in the two world wars parts of the Army swiftly appropriated the enemy's attempt to diminish them by proudly calling themselves The Old Contemptibles and The Desert Rats; and labels like pommy and limey are accepted with a shrug.

Partly as a result of this abusive language, Britain has a reputation for vying with the French as the greatest xenophobes, but this is unfair. Apart from the thugs with IQs about on a level with their ages who beat up immigrants for fun, Britons do not hate foreigners. They despise them.

But even that is beginning to crumble in the face of reality, and modern attitudes are having to change to cope with circumstances. Once, foreigners could be scorned for their incompetence and poverty but many now earn more than the British; they could once be mocked for their pathetic attempts to master English but many now speak it with a flawless fluency that mocks

British failure to acquire more than a 'Good day' plus a few choice expletives in their tongues; and once foreigners could be caricatured from behind the safe refuge of a wall of ignorance but now we come into daily contact with so many of them.

As the European Community continues to increase trade and lower barriers, contact with Europe is bound to accelerate. The trend towards more elaborate business links will continue despite the best efforts of politicians to help it along, and irrespective of the mess they make of treaties and monetary arrangements. Even for the most entrenched of chauvinists this need not be wholly a threat: there are wonderful opportunities for exploitation in the fine old traditions of the empire.

The most obvious and immediate opportunity is to scavenge Europe for cheap labour. You can do this by recruiting the unemployed from eastern Germany, Portugal and Greece and bringing them to Britain where the flexible employment laws make hiring and redundancy much easier. Or you can export the work to other countries, including outside the EC into eastern Europe where labour is cheap, overheads low and morals flexible. After all, the rule for any major international company is to have the work done in the lowest cost country and make profits in the lowest tax country.

As the EC continues to integrate despite misgivings and governments, contacts with overseas countries will continue to grow. And there are enormous opportunities for exploitation further east in the lands recently liberated from communism, where there is an eager enthusiasm to become more capitalist and developed and where there is lots of aid money to spend.

All this dictates a set of new strategies. One has to learn to communicate

with foreigners whether as employees, suppliers or customers and in some cases also as investors.

Tactics for executives Learn at least a bit of the languages you are likely to have to use in business regularly, especially those in which you will have to negotiate. No heroic efforts of education are required – it is not comprehensive or colloquial command that is needed, just enough to get the drift of what is being said. The point is not to use it, at least during negotiations. On the contrary, the whole point is that one must never, except in the direst emergency, disclose the faintest hint of understanding. You face the other side while waiting for the interpreter perhaps allowing the merest smile of eager anticipation to flicker with courtesy across your face; you listen to the struggles of the other side to put complex points into an unfamiliar language with patient encouragement.

This policy may convince them of your ignorance sufficiently to enable you to pick up cautious asides and the private chats of the negotiators, plus the mistakes, inadvertent and intentional, of the interpreter.

The corollary is that you must never be fooled by the other side's pretending not to speak English. Everybody speaks English – it is a well-known fact – and that is why Britons and Americans abroad merely raise their voices to benighted foreigners to show they will not accept obstructionism. So if you are engaged in extensive discussions never mention private opinions or talk about policies and tactics if the opponents can overhear.

The European Community
First lesson is that, since we are now all expected to be committed to

Money is like manure – you have to spread it around or it smells

eventual political convergence or whatever, you must no longer refer to it as the Common Market – the market part of it was merely the broad avenue leading to greater unity. After twenty-five years it was reckoned safe to admit this, but then it has been going since 1958. And in fact the EC's roots are even older than that, having started sprouting in 1947 with the Organisation for Economic Co-operation to apportion Marshall Plan aid, the 1948 Benelux customs union, and the 1952 European Coal and Steel Community.

Despite the antiquity, Britain has not even come close to reconciling itself to the implications of membership. Part of the reason is that Britons fear the EC's imposing another level of bureaucracy on top of the mistrusted meddlers of Whitehall, and another level of politicians to take the point of decision yet further from the people and problems affected.

Brussels has certainly done its best to fuel such fears with fatuous bursts of homogenisation in a fog of Orders, Directives, Regulations and Schedules. Oddly, however, it is the beneficent intentions of such efforts which raise the most fervent petty nationalism – the attempt to make English beaches clean, the insistence that British chocolate contains not just cheap vegetable additives but cocoa, and that sausages contain some meat and not merely offal and cereal.

This does show however that the organisations which comprise the EC do mean well and are keen to improve the lot of everybody, whether they like it or not, and this benign if misguided meddling can be harnessed for personal ends. Show the Eurocrats a Good Cause and they will finance it with all the generous enthusiasm of men doling out somebody else's money.

The European Investment Bank lent 15 billion ecus in 1991 and that has

116

been growing at fifteen per cent a year. The European Bank for Reconstruction and Development was given £10 billion, not all of which has been spent on its premises or its first president's good life. This latter is part of additional funds to shore up labile east European economies, both to prevent social collapse and to avoid ethnic strife. The Community's own budget grew from 4.5 billion ecus in 1973 to 62.5 billion by 1992, with `structural funds' accounting for by far the largest portion of that growth.

These institutions will happily back projects purporting to help the poor who are reckoned to make up a quarter of the EC's population, areas of disintegrating Victorian industry, and scientific research which promises to help Europe catch up with the US and Japan.

Instances of the technological backing are the Forecasting and Assessment in Science and Technology, going nowhere FAST since 1978; the European Strategic Programme for Information Technology set up in 1984 with more ESPRIT than sense; and Research and Development in Advanced Communications Technology for Europe, which has been losing the RACE since 1987. There is a thing called BRITE and there is also backing for biotechnology. Between them these have swallowed almost 10 billion ecus without producing any apparent benefit.

In addition there is of course the notorious agricultural policy, as well as attempts to regulate and reorganise steel, energy, transport, fisheries, the environment, consumer protection, and to impose equality of opportunity.

Tactics for executives   All this combines a heady mixture of eager benevolence, massive amounts of cash and patchy controls which provides two wonderful areas of opportunity.

Firstly, it is a pretty dim manager who cannot milk some of the money for a pet project which will provide employment, salary justification, a lavish entertainment allowance, and kudos for himself and the company. With only a minimal piece of manipulation industrialists can get support for investment, and service businesses get backing for consultancy from one of the innumerable do-gooding budgets.

Secondly, it provides employment opportunities. Brussels is teeming with barely-employed officials: in 1990 there were 24,000 of them, and the 1992 rates of pay were between £13,500 for an unskilled worker and £100,000 for the director general, plus perks such as family allowance, free education for children, and fourteen per cent expatriation allowance. On top of that there are quangos, plus a cloud of lobbyists and support organisations. The Eurocrats get reasonable salaries, good expenses, and pay twenty-five per cent maximum tax; the consultants, lobbyists and trade organisations get even higher pay and enormous entertainment allowances.

When politicians talk of not missing the EC train, they are referring to a gravy train.

For Further Reference

Recruitment pp2–16

(1) 'The situation looks bleak for those employers who fail to change their ways and are slow to look for non-traditional methods of recruitment as well as innovative forms of employment.' B. Curnow – 'Recruit, Retrain, Retain: personnel management and the three Rs', *Personnel Management*, November 1989.

(2) C. Northcote Parkinson – *Parkinson's Law or the pursuit of progress*, 1957.

(3) J. Cannon – *Cost Effective Personnel Decisions*, Institute of Personnel Management, 1979.

(4) R. F. Wagner – 'The Employment Interview: a critical appraisal', *Personnel Psychology* vol 2, 1949; E. Sydney and M. Brown – *The Skills of Interviewing*, Tavistock, 1961; E. C. Webster – *Decision Making in the Employment Interview*, McGill University, 1964; T. Morgan – 'Recent Insights into the Selection Interview', *Personnel Review*, winter 1973; F. M. Lopez – *Personnel Interviewing*, McGraw-Hill, 1975; Derek Torrington and Laura Hall – *Personnel Management*, Prentice Hall, 1991.

(5) Texts which have doubts about either the validity of such tests or about what they find include M. L. Gross – *The Brain Watchers*, Random House, 1962; B. Hoffman – *The Tyranny of Testing*, Crowell-Collier, 1962; H. Black – *They Shall Not Pass*, Morrow, 1963; O. G. Brim – 'American Attitudes Towards Intelligence Tests', *American Psychologist* 20, 1965; L. J. Cronbach – 'Five Decades of Public Controversy Over Mental Testing', *American Psychologist* 30, 1975; W. Haney – 'Validity Vaudeville and Values: a short history of social concerns over standardized testing', *American Psychologist* 36, 1981; L. J. Gould – *The Mismeasure of Man*, Norton, 1981; R. C. Lewontin, S. Rose, L. J. Kamin, *Not In Our Genes*, Pantheon Books, 1984; D. Owen *None of the Above: behind the myth of the scholastic aptitude*, Houghton Mifflin, 1985; M. Snyderman and S. Rothman, 'Survey of Expect Opinion on Intelligence and Aptitude Testing', *American Psychologist* 42 1987.

(6) This is not the cheap jibe it seems. The Max Planck Institute for Psychiatry in Munich spent many years researching the IQs of businessmen acknowledged to be successful and found the distribution of intelligence to be identical with that in the rest of the population. See also similar studies by: L. J. Cronbach, *Essentials of Psychological Testing*, Harper, 1970; D. C. McClelland 'Testing for Competence Rather than for Intelligence,' *American Psychologist* 28 1973.

(7) P. R. Plumbley, *Recruitment and Selection*, Institute of Personnel Management, 1985.

(8) It was in 1905 that Alfred Binet and Theodore Simon started testing Parisian children to see if they needed extra tuition. Lewis Terman of Stanford University revised their tests, which are still in widespread use, and called the Binet-Stanford tests. For adults more common tests are the Wechsler (sometimes called the WAIS-R) and AH4, though a range of others have been devised in attempts to make the testing culture and literacy free. L. J. Horn and G. Y. Donaldson, 'Cognitive Development in Adulthood', in O. G. Brim and J. Kagan (eds) – *Constancy and Change in Human Development*, Harvard University Press, 1980.

(9) John von Neumann and Oskar Morgenstern – *The Theory of Games and Economic Behaviour*, Princeton University Press, 1944.

(10) The great war strategist Karl von Clausewitz said 'in war the will is directed at an animate object that reacts'.

(11) John MacMillan – *Games Strategies and Managers: how managers can use game theory to make better business decisions*, Oxford University Press, 1992.

Performance pp17–29

(1) Fabius Maximus, quoted in Plutarch's *Lives*.

(2) Tom Peters and Robert Waterman – *In Search of Excellence*, Harper, 1982.

(3) Polybius – *Histories*.

(4) In his later book *Liberation Management* Tom Peters himself added that as product lives are shortening large corporations have too great an inertia to respond rapidly enough to survive and so should split themselves into a federation of smaller businesses.

(5) Charles Handy, for instance, advocates flexible structures: 'teams of coalition of influence and power rather than control; leadership not management'. (Charles Handy – *The Age of Unreason*, Business Books, 1989.)

(6) C. Fletcher and R. Williams – *Performance Appraisal and Career Development*, Hutchinson, 1985

(7) G. Randell, P. Packard, J. Slater – *Staff Appraisal*, Institute of Personnel Management, 1984.

(8) Irwin W. Krantz – 'Evaluating the Technical Employee: the results approach', *Personnel* vol 35/3, 1957.

(9) Douglas McGregor – 'The Human Side of the Enterprise', in *Adventures in Thought and Action*, Massachussetts Institute of Technology, 1957.

(10) H. H. Meyer – 'Self-Appraisal of Job Performance', *Personnel Psychology* vol 33, 1980.

(11) G. P. Latham and K N. Wexley – *Increased Productivity Through Performance Appraisal*, Addison Wesley, 1981.

(12) A. F. L. Beech (ed) – *Principles and Practice of Management*, Longman.

(13) Robert Townsend – *Up the Organisation*, Knopf, 1970.

(14) 'A well-wrapped statistic is better than Hitler's "big lie"; it misleads yet it cannot be pinned on you', said Darrell Huff in *How to Lie with Statistics*, Victor Gollancz, 1954.

Discipline pp30–44

(1) Peter Drucker – *Management: tasks, responsibilities, practices*, Harper & Row, 1973.

(2) J. B. Watson – 'Psychology as the Behaviourist Views It', *Psychology Review*, vol 20, 1913. B. F. Skinner – *Science and Human Behaviour*, Macmillan, New York, 1953.

(3) What precisely people want as reward has been debated at length by industrial psychologists. A. H. Maslow explained people have a hierarchy of needs – after they have satisfied the survival needs of food, clothing and shelter, they seek physical safety. When they have all that they turn attention to social needs of belonging, and afterwards they seek status and self-esteem. Finally, with everything else already satisfied, they want to realise their full potential. (A. H. Maslow – 'A Theory of Human Motivation', *Psychological Review* vol 50/4, 1943; A. H. Maslow – *Motivation and Personality*, Harper & Row, 1943.)

(4) G. B. Shaw – *Man and Superman* appendix: 'Maxims for Revolutionists', 1903.

(5) Fred Herzberg – *The Motivation to Work*, Wiley, 1965; Fred Herzberg – *Work and the Nature of Man*, World Publishing, 1966.

(6) Thanks in the main to the book, Richard Pascale and Anthony Athos – *The Art of Japanese Management*, Simon & Schuster, 1981.

(7) Bishop W. C. Magee, sermon at Peterborough, 1868, quoted by E. J. Phelps in a Mansion House Speech, 24 January 1889.

(8) *Taylor v Alidair*, Appeal Court.

(9) *James v Waltham Holy Cross UDC*, 1973, ICR 398.

(10) *International Sports v Thomson*, 1980.

(11) *Rosenthal v Butler*, 1972.

(12) M. Winchup – *Modern Employment Law*, Heinemann, 1976.

(13) *Futty v Breckles*, 1974.

(14) *Walken v Humberside Erection Company*, 1976.

(15) F. J. Roethlisberger and W. J. Dickson – *Management and the Worker*, Harvard University Press, 1939.

(16) Benjamin Selekman – *Labor Relations and Human Relations*, McGraw-Hill, 1947.

(17) Derek Torrington and Laura Hill – *Personnel Management*, Prentice Hall, 1991.

(18) David Moreau – *Look Behind You*, Associated Business Programmes, 1973.

Promotion pp45–61

(1) Quoted in the *New York Times*, 19 January 1971.

(2) L. J. Peter and R. Hull – *The Peter Principle*, 1970.

(3) Charles Handy – *Understanding Organisations*, Penguin, 1985.

(4) *Life*, 1932; though he is supposed to have said it first around 1899. Actually, Thomas Carlyle said a long time even before that, genius was the 'transcendant capacity of taking trouble'.

(5) Ron Coleman and Giles Barrie – *525 Ways to Be A Better Manager*, Gower, 1990.

(6) 'The man-god must be killed as soon as he shows symptoms that his powers are beginning to fail, and his soul must be transferred to a vigorous successor.' J. G. Frazer – *The Golden Bough*, Macmillan, 1922.

(7) 'Organisations are political systems in which those who understand power and politics win.' John W. Hunt – *Managing People at Work*, McGraw-Hill, 1992.

(8) John Stuart Mill said the notion that truth prevails 'is one of those pleasant falsehoods which men repeat after one another till they pass into commonplaces but which all experience refutes'.

(9) Douglas McGregor – *The Human Side of the Enterprise*, McGraw-Hill, 1960. The idea probably came from Peter Drucker – *Concept of the Corporation*, John Day, 1946, and the pyramid of human wants (which McGregor used as the reward/punishment scale to accompany his binary system) derived from A. H. Maslow – 'A Theory of Human Motivation', *Psychological Review* vol 50/4, 1943; Kenneth Blanchard – *The One Minute Manager*, 1983; Edward de Bono – *The Use of Lateral Thinking*, McGraw-Hill, 1967, and at least ten other books on the subject since then; Tom Peters; E. F. Schumacher – *Small Is Beautiful*, Blond & Briggs, 1973.

Training pp62–70

(1) A. M. Pettigrew, P. Sparrow, C. Hendry – 'The Forces that Trigger Training', *Personnel Management*, December 1988.

(2) Derek Torrington and Laura Hall – *Personnel Management*, Prentice Hall, 1991.

(3) A. Rajan and J. Fryatt – *Create or Abdicate: the City's human resource choice for the 90s*, Witherby, 1988; National Economic Development Office – *Competence and Competition*, HMSO 1984.

(4) As pretty well a random example, the scientist Lyon Playfair in 1867 said what has been echoed so frequently since. 'France, Prussia, Austria, Belgium and Switzerland possess good systems of industrial education for the masters and managers of factories and workshops, and England possesses none.'

(5) Derek Torrington and Laura Hall – *Personnel Management*, Prentice Hall, 1991.

(6) Research on Japanese industrialists in Kenichi Ohmae in *The Mind of the Strategist*, McGraw-Hill, 1982; 'The business schools in the US, set up less than a century ago, have been preparing well-trained clerks.' Peter

Drucker – *The Age of Discontinuity*, 1969. 'Some pretty fundamental requirements for success: humility, respect for people in the firing line; deep understanding of the nature of business and the kind of people who can enjoy making it prosper; respect from way down the line; a demonstrated record of guts, industry, loyalty, judgment, fairness and honesty under pressure' are all lacking in management graduates: Robert Townsend – *Up the Organisation*, Knopf, 1970

Communications pp71–84

(1) Allan Pease – *Body Language*, Sheldon Press, 1984; Gerard I. Nierenberg and Henry H. Colero – *How to Read a Person Like a Book*, Heinrich Hanau, 1973.
(2) 'The world will never learn to beware of those stately gentlemen with the fixed calm look straight into your eyes, who never joke, and never waver, profuse in cautions and allusions, but practised in rightly-laced silences – which is why the confidence trick is still running.' William Bolitho – *Twelve Against the Gods*.
(3) First set out in a methodical manner is that classic of management textbooks, F. W. Taylor – *Principles of Scientific Management*, Harper, 1911.
(4) J. M. Keynes – *The General Theory of Employment, Interest and Money*, Macmillan, 1936.
(5) One of the most popular was Douglas McGregor – *The Human Side of the Enterprise*, McGraw-Hill, 1960, which contrasted the authoritarian X and libertarian Y types. This really set the fashion which still prevails for assuming that if people take part in setting corporate and personal goals they will become so committed to them that they will work harder than if driven by a supervisor.
(6) Napoleon was making a similar point about both this and vicious compliance in a military context in his book *Military Maxims and Thoughts*: 'A commander in chief cannot excuse his mistakes in war

as an order from his minister or sovereign, when the person giving the order is away from the field of operations and is partly or wholly unaware of the latest circumstances. It follows that a commander who carries out a plan he considers is faulty is culpable: he must put forward his reasons, insist on the plan being changed and finally offer his resignation rather than be an instrument of the army's downfall.'
(7) Peter Drucker – *Management: tasks, responsibilities, practices*, Harper & Row, 1973.
(8) Rensis Likert – *New Patterns of Management*, McGraw-Hill, 1961; Rensis Likert – *The Human Organisation*, McGraw-Hill, 1967.
(9) C. Argyris – 'Interpersonal Barriers to Decision Making', *Harvard Business Review*.
(10) Chris Argyris & D. A. Schon – *Organisational Learning: a theory of action perspective*, Addison Wesley, 1978.
(11) Val R. Lorwin in his book *The French Labour Movement*, Harvard University Press, 1954, described most work in industrial relations as suffering from the Pago-Pago fallacy: describing everything like 'a South Sea island, in terms of what is strange and different', instead of what is familiar and well understood.

Pay pp85–96

(1) Elliott Jaques – 'Objective Measures for Pay Differentials', *Harvard Business Review* Jan/Feb 1962.
(2) C. Northcote Parkinson – *The Law and the Profits*, 1960.
(3) *Strategikon*, c. AD 600.

Working Environment pp97–103

(1) The full list deserves to be studied:
 1. directors drive Rolls-Royces with personalised number plates
 2. fountain in the reception area
 3. flagpole outside the factory
 4. Queen's Award for industry
 5. chairman honoured for services to industry
 6. salesman or engineer as chief executive
 7. new offices opened by prime minister
 8. unqualified or elderly accountant
 9. products are market leaders
 10. 'Hi-Tec' included in corporate name
 11. audit partner grew up with the company
 12. chairman is politician or well known for charitable works
 13. satisfied personnel with no strike record
 14. recently announced technological break-through
 15. whizz-kid as vice-chairman
 16. company received Accountant award for best report and accounts
 17. annual report shows chairman getting out of helicopter
 They have been published in many places, including *Accountancy Age*, December 1984.
(2) C. Northcote Parkinson – *Parkinson's Law or the pursuit of progress*, US, 1957.
(3) Elton Mayo – *The Human Problems of an Industrial Civilisation*, Macmillan, 1933.
(4) Laws governing the workplace include: Factories Act 1961; Offices Shops and Railway Premises Act 1963; Employers' Liability (Compulsory Insurance) Act 1969; Employers' Liability (Defective Equipment) Act 1969; Fire Precautions Act 1971; Health and Safety at Work Act 1974; plus innumerable regulations, many issued under those Acts.
(5) *Smith v Austin Lifts*, 1959, 1 All ER 81
(6) I. Keil – 'Advice to Magnates: management education in the thirteenth century', *Bulletin of the Association of Teachers in Management 17*, March 1965, reckons the first English textbook on the subject was by Robert Grosseteste – *The Rules of St Robert*.
(7) 'The literature leaves one with the impression that after all not a great deal has been said about organisations, but it has been said over and over in a variety

of languages.' James G. March and Herbert A. Simon – *Organizations*, Wiley, 1958.

(8) 'More and more organisations are finding that the ways of the future cannot be systematically planned, new products, techniques and methods do not always succumb to logic even if backed by massive resources. There is therefore a growing respectability for more experimentation and for more free-form types of structure.' Charles Handy – *Understanding Organisations*, Penguin 1985.

Staff Turnover pp104–112

(1) In *McNeil v Charles Crimin (Electrical Contractors)* 1984, Mr McNeil, a foreman, was told to work under the supervision of an ordinary electrician. In *Marriot v Oxford Cooperative Society*, 1970, a foreman successfully fought off a cut in pay and status.

(2) In *Robinson v Crompton Parkinson*, 1978, an unjustified accusation was held to have breached the 'relationship of trust and confidence' that should exist between employer and employee.

(3) In *Palmanor v Cedron* 1978, the nightclub manager swore spectacularly at one of his workmen and said if he did not like it he could leave. He did just that and then successfully sued with the court deciding the language had been not just unreasonable but so appalling it went to the root of the employment contract.

(4) In *Jones v Wadham Stringer*, 1983, a fleet sales director was gradually demoted and shunted into ever more cramped offices with less furniture and fewer facilities.

(5) *Simmons v Dowty Seals*, 1978.